D1565223

THE
CODEPENDENT
COUNSELOR

THE CODEPENDENT COUNSELOR

Guidelines
for Self-
Assessment
and
Change

Philip J. Beebe

Foreword by
TERENCE T. GORSKI

Based on the CENAPS Model of Treatment

"Diagnostic Criteria for Codependent Personality Disorder" from *Diagnosing and Treating Co-Dependence* by Timmen L. Cermak (Minneapolis, Minn.: Johnson Institute, 1986). Used by permission of the Johnson Institute.

"Styles of Enabling Behavior," TREATING COCAINE DEPENDENCY by David E. Smith, M.D., and Donald R. Wesson, M.D., copyright 1988, by Hazelden Foundation, Center City, Minnesota. Reprinted by permission.

"Characteristic Behaviors of the Addictive Process," CO-DEPENDENCE: MISUNDER-STOOD—MISTREATED by Anne Wilson Schaef (New York, Harper & Row, 1986). Reprinted by permission.

"Children of Alcoholics Screening Test (CAST)," copyright © 1983 by John W. Jones, Ph.D. All rights reserved. Used by permission of Camelot Unlimited, Chicago.

J. Friel, "Co-Dependency Assessment Inventory," *Focus On Chemically Dependent Families* 8 (Deerfield Beach, Florida: 1985): 20-21. Reprinted with permission from *Focus* magazine.

Published by:
Herald House/Independence Press
P.O. Box 390
Independence, MO 64051-0390
1-800-767-8181 or 816/521-3015

Printed in the United States of America

Library of Congress Cataloging-in-Publication Data
Beebe, Philip J.
 The Codependent Counselor: Guidelines for Self-assessment and Change / Philip J. Beebe ; foreword by Terence T. Gorski.
     p.   cm.
ISBN 0-8309-0560-X
 1. Counseling. 2. Counselor and client. 3. Co-dependence (Psychology) 4. Narcotic addicts—Counseling of. 5. Alcoholism—Counseling of. 6. Substance abuse—Treatment. I. Title.
BF637.C6B335   1990
362.29'13—dc20   90-42129
                                                       CIP

Contents

List of Figures

Questionnaires/Screening Instruments

Foreword

The rapid emergence of the codependence field has both excited and frightened me. I am excited by the dynamic growth of programs that help people recover from the effects of dysfunctional relationships. For the first time in history people who have been damaged can come out of the closet. The message is clear: "It is not your fault! You are not to blame! You *can* recover!" With this rallying cry, literally millions of people have formed a recovery "army" dedicated to ending the growing epidemic of family and relationship dysfunctions. This army carries a banner that says, 'We can break the cycle of family dysfunction." And they mean it. Millions of adult Americans are seeking recovery by using Twelve Step groups, professional therapy, or a combination of both. They sincerely say, "I won't do to my children what was done to me!"

My concern has been with the confusion and mystification of codependence and its treatment. The confusion stems from the fact that even the experts can't agree on exactly what codependence is and how it should be treated. The mystification occurs because many recovering people — a lot of them therapists — have an almost religious fervor when dealing with the issues of codependence. They are true believers in the movement even though they are not clear about what they believe in. "I don't want to think about it too much," one counselor told me. "Codependency treatment has saved my life. I'm feeling good for the first time. I don't want to ruin those good feelings by intellectualizing my experience. I just want to share my own experience in recovery!"

In an effort to recover, many people have failed to find a balance between the child within and their rational adult side. As a result some segments of the codependence field have developed in isolation from established psychological and family therapy. New terms have been created and used with little effort to relate those terms to existing theories and concepts. This has led the codependence movement to "recreate the wheel" and simply call it something else. For example, many aspects of codependence treatment are a repeat of the encounter and human potential movements of the 1960s. Many "new" forms of therapy for codependence are actually a reintroduction of Gestalt and experiential techniques that proved to have limited effectiveness during the 1960s but are being dusted off and applied to recovering codependents in the 1980s and 1990s.

There is no doubt that the personal problems of therapists and counselors can and often do interfere with patient care and the efficient operation of treatment programs. Many of these problems are caused by the therapists' unresolved issues from childhood that drive them to help others for all the wrong reasons. Many therapists are motivated by unconscious beliefs like, "Since I couldn't help my mother or father, I must help everyone else," or "I must help others to avoid the kind of pain and dysfunction that I experienced." Because they are motivated by their own unresolved problems, many of these therapists lose perspective and actually hurt the patients they are trying to help.

The term codependence is relatively new and is often used to describe people who have problems with obsessive caretaking and people helping. Unfortunately, the exact meaning of the term has become confused. This confusion is making it difficult for counselors, therapists, and supervisors to deal effectively with family-of-origin problems that interfere with the professional performance of counselors and therapists.

In an effort to sort out this confusion, I explored the history of the term codependence. Here is what I found. Shortly after the founding of Alcoholics Anonymous (AA) in 1935, it was recognized that adults who live in committed relationships with alcoholics were damaged by those relationships. This damage was originally referred to as **co-alcoholism**. In the early 1940s AA Family Group Meetings, which later grew into Alanon, were organized to meet the needs of co-alcoholics (Alanon, 1979). In the later 1960s and early 1970s treatment centers began to develop programs for families of alcoholics. At first these programs were directed toward enlisting the support of family members in keeping alcoholic patients sober (NIAAA, 1981; NIAAA, 1987). The focus of these programs gradually shifted to meeting the needs of the co-alcoholics themselves. Co-alcoholism began to emerge as a separate diagnostic category.

Awareness began to grow that children raised by alcoholic parents suffered more severe and long-lasting damage than adults who were raised in nonalcoholic homes and later married alcoholics. A distinction was made between co-alcoholics (adults from nonalcoholic families who later married alcoholics) and para-alcoholics (children who were raised by alcoholic parents). The specific damage to children was discussed under the term **adult children of alcoholics**. Because this damage persisted into adulthood, the term adult children of alcoholics came into widespread use. A Twelve Step support group named Adult Children of Alcoholics (ACOA) was developed in the early 1980s and grew rapidly.

In the late 1970s the term chemical dependence came into widespread use and the term alcoholism was conceptualized as a type of chemical dependence. As a result the term co-alcoholic was generalized to the term codependent. As the ACOA movement grew the term codependent was used to describe both adults who were damaged by marrying chemically dependent partners and children who were damaged by chemically dependent parents. As more clinical observations were made of codependents (adults and children damaged by chemical dependence) it became apparent that people who were damaged by living in committed relationships with chemical addicts did not differ significantly from people damaged by living in committed relationships with other dysfunctional people. The term codependent was expanded again to account for all people who have been damaged by living in a relationship with a dysfunctional person regardless of the cause of the dysfunction. The term **adult children from dysfunctional families (ACDF)** began to be utilized.

As efforts were made to describe the personality characteristics of codependents (now used to describe people damaged by any dysfunctional behavior of another person) it was discovered that some, but not all, had a personality that was organized around low self-esteem, obsessive involvement with others in order to raise self-esteem, and extreme caretaking behavior that resulted in lack of self-care. This observation caused many people to begin using the term codependence to describe that particular personality style.

So it seems that the current usage of the term codependence involves four distinctly different definitions. In the first, codependence is defined as a cluster of symptoms or maladaptive behavior changes that occur in

adults who live in a committed relationship with a chemically dependent person. This definition of codependence would fit those who typically choose Alanon as a primary source of recovery. In the second, codependence is defined as a cluster of symptoms or maladaptive behavior changes that occur in **children who are raised by chemically dependent parents.** This definition of codependence would fit those who typically choose ACOA as a primary source of recovery. In the third, codependence is defined as a cluster of symptoms or maladaptive behavior changes associated with living in a committed relationship with **a chemically dependent person or a chronically dysfunctional person either as children or adults.** This definition would fit those who identify with the concept of ACDF. The fourth definition defines codependence as a specific **pattern of personality traits** that are characterized by loss of self-identity, over-involvement with others as a means of establishing self-identity, and excessive caretaking behavior that results in a lack of self-care.

In trying to use the concept of codependence in counselor training, I created a system of definitions that readily differentiates between these four different meanings. In this system the term **codependent** is defined as a general term describing a cluster of symptoms or maladaptive behavior changes associated with living in a committed relationship with either a chemically dependent person or a chronically dysfunctional person either as children or adults.

Codependence is then specified as having various types. A **codependent adjustment reaction** is a type of codependence characterized by the spontaneous remission of codependent symptoms when the person is no longer in the committed relationship with the chemically dependent or chronically dysfunctional person. A **codependent disorder** is a type of codependence characterized by the continuation of codependent symptoms even when the person is no longer in a committed relationship with the chemically dependent or chronically dysfunctional person. **Child onset codependence** is a type of codependence (either codependent adjustment reaction or codependent disorder) that is caused by being raised in an addictive or dysfunctional family of origin. **Adult onset codependence is a type of codependence (either codependent adjustment reaction or codependent disorder) that is caused by being involved in a committed relationship as an adult with an addicted or dysfunctional person.**

Adult onset codependence can result in two forms of self-defeating personality styles: the counterdependent and the codependent. The **counterdependent (manipulative) personality** is a specific pattern of personality traits that are characterized by excessive preoccupation with self and the excessive use of intrusive and manipulative behavior as a means of establishing self-identity. The **codependent (caretaking) personality** is a specific pattern of personality traits that are characterized by loss of self-identity, over-involvement with others as a means of establishing self-identity, and excessive caretaking behavior that results in a lack of self-care. Both codependents and noncodependents can exhibit a caretaking personality.

A severity scale can be used with the above definitions to describe a range of intensity of problems from mild to severe. **Mild codependent symptoms** produce subjective distress but create no social or occupational impairment. **Moderate codependent symptoms** produce subjective distress and create minimal social and occupational impairment. **Severe codependent symptoms** produce subjective distress and create substantial social or occupational impairment.

To classify a patient as codependent using this nomenclature would involve answering a series of diagnostic questions. The first question is, "Has this person been damaged as a consequence of living in a committed relationship with a substance user or other dysfunctional person?" If the answer is yes, the person meets the general definition of codependence and the second question is answered. If the answer is no, the person does not have a problem with codependence.

The second question is, "Did this damage first occur when this person was a child?" If the answer is yes, the person meets the criteria of child onset codependence. If the answer is no, the person meets the criteria of adult onset codependence.

The third question is, "Have the maladaptive behaviors been internalized to the point that they are acted out independently of the specific relationship in which they were created?" If the answer is yes, the person meets the criteria of a codependent disorder. If the answer is no, the person meets the criteria of a codependent adjustment reaction.

The last three questions define the severity of the codependence. The fourth question is, "Do the symptoms produce subjective distress but no social or occupational impairment?" If the answer is yes, the person has mild symptoms. The fifth question is, "Do the symptoms produce subjective distress that creates minimal social and occupational impairment?" If the answer is yes, the person has moderate symptoms. The final question is, "Do the symptoms produce subjective distress and create substantial social or occupational impairment?'' If the answer is yes, the person has severe codependence.

I then became intrigued with the relationship of chemical dependence and codependence. In researching this subject I found that approximately 60 percent of all chemically dependent patients entering treatment for the first time (Hoffman and Harrison, 1986) and 90 percent of all chronically relapse-prone patients were raised in alcoholic family systems and would be appropriately described as having a multiple diagnosis of chemical dependence and child onset codependence. This high rate of multiple diagnosis has led to confusion about the relationship between codependence and chemical dependence.

If we use the definition of codependence as symptoms resulting from damage caused by living in a committed relationship with a chemically dependent or dysfunctional person, there would be two possible relationships between codependence and chemical dependence. Codependence could cause chemical dependence or codependence and chemical dependence could be coexisting disorders that have no causative relationship but do interact dynamically with each other.

There is substantial evidence that codependence (i.e., being raised in a dysfunctional family) does not cause chemical dependence, but it can cause serious complications to recovery that can interfere with recovery and increase the risk of relapse (Gorski, 1989).

Therefore, codependence and chemical dependence appear to be independent conditions that often coexist. Being chemically dependent does not cause a person to develop codependence. Being codependent does not cause a person to develop chemical dependence. Many people suffer from codependence and chemical dependence at the same time. The presence of one can interfere with recovery from the other.

The next issue was how to appropriately treat people suffering from both chemical dependence and codependence. I developed three simple guidelines: (1) bring the chemical dependence into remission first through a program of abstinence, detoxification, and the development of a recovery program; (2) treat severe codependence issues that increase the risk of relapse to chemical dependence early in the recovery process; and (3) treat the less severe codependence issues in late recovery after a stable sobriety program has been established.

My final step was to attempt to relate my new understanding of codependence to the established psychological literature and then develop programs for applying that information to the codependent counselor and therapist. This is when Philip Beebe sent his manuscript, "The Codependent Counselor," for review. I was struggling to understand the complexities of the codependence movement and how it applied to the treatment of chemical dependence. This book clearly demonstrates that many of the problems in the codependence field have been caused because well-meaning and dedicated therapists have plunged ahead to save the world from codependence without first establishing a recovery program for themselves.

I found Mr. Beebe's ideas to be helpful because he clearly stated current definitions and treatment methods for codependence and went one step further. He related those theories and techniques to the established psychological literature. Also, he developed concrete recommendations for how treatment centers and individual therapists can effectively address the problem of codependence. All of this he presented in a friendly, warm, and easy-to-read manner.

Taking a systematic and scholarly approach to the issue of the codependent counselor, Mr. Beebe has created a compassionate, yet academically sound approach to identifying and managing codependence in the professional counselor or therapist. Much of what he says can be applied to the treatment of any codependent. The book describes the effect of codependence on clinical performance and provides a useful tool for self-examination and clinical performance appraisal. The book ends with a series of practical guidelines for growth and change.

What is needed in the codependence field today is an academically sound and no-nonsense approach to understanding codependence, its impact on the professional counselor, and effective approaches for treatment and clinical supervision. I believe Philip Beebe's book provides all of these elements and clearly demonstrates that codependence can be understood and effectively integrated with traditional counseling and therapy techniques.

This is a book that will be read and enjoyed by counselors and therapists using a variety of philosophies and theories. It provides a wealth of valuable academic resources and is essential for anyone who is seriously interested in how codependence affects counselors and therapists and what can be done about it. I strongly recommend *The Codependent Counselor* as must reading for all chemical dependence and codependence therapists.

Terence T. Gorski
March 1990

Bibliography

Alanon, *Louis Remembers, Memoirs of the Cofounder of Alanon and Wife of the Cofounder of Alcoholics Anonymous*. New York: Alanon Group Headquarters, Inc., 1979.

Gorski, Terence T., *Do Family of Origin Problems Cause Chemical Addiction? Exploring the Relationship Between Chemical Dependence and Codependence*. Independence, Missouri: Herald House/Independence Press, 1989.

Hoffman, N. G. and P. A. Harrison, *CATOR 1986 Report, Findings Two Years After Treatment*. St. Paul, Minnesota: CATOR (Chemical Abuse Treatment Outcome Registry), 1986.

NIAAA, *Sixth Special Report to the U. S. Congress on Alcohol and Health*. Rockville, Maryland: National Institute on Alcohol Abuse and Alcoholism, January 1987.

NIAAA, *Fourth Special Report to the U. S. Congress on Alcohol and Health*. Rockville, Maryland: National Institute on Alcohol Abuse and Alcoholism, January 1981.

Preface

Early in my career I learned a hard lesson. Many of the problems I had with my patients were my problems, not theirs. When I "got hooked" by those problems it was my own unresolved history, not the client, that was hooking me. This wasn't an easy lesson to learn. While working as a Navy Alcohol and Drug Abuse Counselor I became increasingly aware that I had more difficulties working with some clients than with others.

With some patients I tended to overreact, while I could stay calm and professional with others. At times when I overreacted I would need several hours and a long conversation with a colleague to calm down and get a perspective on what had happened. I knew I had got hooked by the client. A part of me knew it was my problem; another part of me blamed the client. These incidents left me feeling inadequate and incompetent. And worst of all, I didn't understand what was happening or why.

During some of my periods of self-examination, I was able to see that my responses in a given situation were due to personal issues rather than what the client had said or done. Over time, I found that more and more of these incidents could be tracked to issues about my past experiences and that

I had been "hooked,"
not by the client
but by my own history.

I was also confused by the fact that some of my peers never seemed to have such problems with their clients and never had to search out the causes for interpersonal difficulties. They always seemed so certain of their assessments and recommendations that I wondered if

21

there was something wrong with me and my abilities to work as a counselor.

Since I felt that I needed to learn more about counseling and to improve my own techniques and skills, I began to attend workshops, seminars, and classes on the subject. Whenever the opportunity presented itself, I used my own fears, personal issues, and problems as material for the class rather than role playing a situation. This allowed me to begin to gain insight into myself. I was able to hone my own abilities and sensitivities so that I could start to see that in fact I had not done as badly as I had thought.

By doing this, I began to see that my peers were not always as correct as they presented themselves and that, in fact, some of their assessments had missed the true problem because they too had been "hooked." I also began to see that the "hooks" were more often their own issues rather than the material presented by the client. I was able to begin to identify and point out the issues that they were "hooked" on. Sometimes these discussions were successful, but more frequently my colleagues responded with rationalizations and denial. I could not understand why they did not seem as willing to examine their issues as I was to look at my own weaknesses.

When I took a new job working in a multiple-offender drinking driver program I continued to examine my own personal and professional issues. One of the things I rapidly came to understand was that I was inadequately prepared to deal with the range of problems presented by my clients. As a result, I decided that I needed to return to school for additional formal training in counseling.

Before I left that job to return to school, however, I had to deal with the same events that had affected me when I worked for the Navy. My own feelings of incompetence, inadequacy, and insecurity made me feel less effective than I wanted to be. I was frequently amused when the Program Director would "assign" Al-Anon meetings to herself or one of her counselors following some event in which a client had been allowed to violate program rules without being held to account for the consequences and the counselor had assumed the responsibility for the client.

After a while, I came to see that, while the assignment of Al-Anon meetings was made somewhat tongue-in-cheek, the diagnosis of codependent behavior was accurate. As I looked around at my peers and others I knew in the counseling field, I saw that codependent behaviors were common in them. My own past experiences as a counselor showed me that the diagnosis was probably accurate for me as well.

When I returned to school, I chose to focus on codependency as found in the therapeutic relationship. In a very short period of time, I found that it was not a common topic for research. There were some anecdotal reports and informal studies of codependency in the helping professions, frequently associated with discussions of the career choices made by Adult Children of Alcoholics. I was unable to find any well documented studies of the prevalence of codependency in therapists or the counseling relationship. I also found that in order for the concept of codependency to receive the general acceptance needed in the larger therapeutic community, it would be necessary to establish a valid base in current psychological theory and remove codependency from the narrow confines of the chemical dependency field.

When discussing my topic with other students, I received enthusiastic support from them as well as requests to use my work as resource material for their research. In our discussions, I learned about their own experiences with codependency in their internships and the lack of supervision they received about it. I also received such comments as "That's really needed, but I don't think I want to read it." As I completed my studies, I became convinced that the issue of counselor codependency is in fact of vital importance.

During my research for a thesis and then during subsequent rewrites, I had to examine my own issues of codependency both personally and professionally. I began to work through some of the residue of my earlier problems with my own therapeutic codependency as well as some of that of former peers. I have learned the dangers to myself of being a professional codependent in the process of studying this phenomenon.

I am coming to believe that codependency in a therapist is potentially one of the most severe impairments that a professional can experience because of the possible severe effects on so many different people. I also believe that this problem is one that can be resolved or at least minimized with the appropriate education, recovery programs, and supervision.

The concept of the "Wounded Healer" has been discussed from C. G. Jung to the pages of *Atlantic* magazine. If the impairment is codependency, the "wounded healer" can take some positive actions which can make a significant difference in the recovery process.

Philip J. Beebe

Acknowledgments

I wish to express my gratitude to those individuals who intentionally or unknowingly aided me tremendously in the completion of this project. First, Dolores Bicknell, of the Post Conviction Drinking Driver Program in Contra Costa County, California, whose frequent referrals of her staff to Al-Anon gave rise to my original thoughts on this subject. Many of my co-workers in the field of alcoholism and drug abuse counseling have added to my awareness of the problem and the possible extent of it.

I am grateful for the guidance provided by both of my advisers, Dr. Thomas Soldahl and Dr. Robert White of California State University–Hayward, in the writing of this project. My classmates at that university have provided both examples and ideas during our frequent discussions.

Finally, my everlasting gratitude goes to my partner, Elaine Funaro, for her continual emotional support and encouragement in this entire effort. Her questions and arguments helped me avoid numerous tangents and therefore stay on track.

Chapter 1

Therapeutic Relationships

Tom M., Program Director

My name is Tom M. I am the program director of the fictional High Hopes Chemical Dependency Treatment Program. My program provides a wide range of services to alcoholics and addicts with both an inpatient and an outpatient component. My agency is well respected because we have always provided high quality services to our clients and patients.

I have been fortunate in being able to bring together a treatment team which has been clearly superior to any other in our area. I have twelve clinical counselors, two clerical assistants, two admissions counselors, and a receptionist as members of my staff. All of them have worked for me for at least three years. Additionally, the program has a nursing staff and a community relations/ outreach staff. These two components are not directly supervised by me.

Two of my most effective counselors are Mary G. and

Sam T. Mary has been on the staff for about eight years and provides group and individual counseling services for clients in the outpatient program. Sam works in the inpatient department and is most actively involved in groups with some individual counseling.

Recently I noticed that problems with clients and staff have been on the increase and I am beginning to get increasingly concerned about this situation. So far I haven't been able to identify any particular causes for the difficulties, but I am still struggling with trying to make sense of the problems. I know that the work of Sam and Mary has been affected and this is important to the effectiveness of the program.

Mary has recently experienced a series of minor illnesses which have resulted in her being away from work for a considerable period of time. She has also become increasingly irritable with other staff members and seems less efficient in her work performance. So far things have not gotten to the point that I have said anything to her, but I am really getting concerned about her. She rarely, if ever, lets me or anyone else know what is happening in her private or professional life and I am concerned about what might be happening and how that might affect others here at work.

Sam also is presenting behaviors which are of concern to me. He is becoming very defensive about some of his clients' progress in treatment. He is also spending more time at work with no significant increase in output. Sam is much less approachable by his co-workers than he was in previous months and he tends to disappear into his office on breaks rather than mingle with other staff. Since he is recovering, I talked with him once about the possibility of a relapse, but he assured me that everything was okay for him, that he didn't have any problem, and that he just wanted to take care of the other things in his own way.

My administrative staff is complaining more about the clinical staff than they used to and, furthermore, I have noticed that they frequently stop talking when I approach. They used to be willing to sit and talk with me and that has stopped. Their work output is still satisfactory, but I keep getting complaints from the clinical staff and clients about the attitudes of the receptionist and clerical workers.

The nursing staff at the inpatient unit is a frequent source of conflict between patients and staff—a situation which occasionally makes it necessary for the counselors to spend extra time focused on those interpersonal problems. It seems as if Susan, the nursing supervisor, is no longer as approachable as she once was to discuss problems with the nursing staff. She just says that it is hard to get good nurses and not to bother her, she has problems of her own.

I feel more and more discouraged about my ability to carry out the responsibilities of this job. Everyone tells me that these kinds of problems never happened under the former program director. Sometimes I wonder if I should resign my position and then all of these problems would resolve themselves. I really wish that the solution to all of these little headaches would suddenly appear to me in my sleep so that I could apply the needed corrections and everything would work smoothly again.

I find myself spending many hours at home trying to find solutions to the situation. Any one of the things by itself is not a major problem and I could handle it with no difficulty. Right now, there are so many things happening that I just don't know where to start. Besides, everything I have tried just isn't working, and I don't understand why.

I have decided to hire an outside consultant to help me figure out what is going on here. I think that may be what is needed to get this situation ironed out. Anyway, he is going to work on a strategy for intervention in the agency.

This book examines the actively codependent therapist, a dysfunctional aspect of the counseling relationship which would seem more common than many may realize. From the field of alcoholism counseling and treatment comes the concept of co-alcoholism. Originally focused on an alcoholic relationship, this concept has grown to incorporate relationships involving any drug addiction or dependency and now includes those relationships which involve other problems. The concept is moving out of strictly dysfunctional relationships and into the area of all interpersonal behaviors. "Codependency" seems to have replaced co-alcoholism as the term of choice in the chemical dependency field (Cermak, 1986a; Schaef, 1986; Wegscheider-Cruse, 1985). With the current wide interest in Adult Children of Alcoholics, the term is moving into other areas of therapy.

Codependency is a pattern of interpersonal behaviors and traits most often seen in those persons who are in chemically dependent or other dysfunctional relationships, primarily in their interactions within that relationship. These traits include difficulty and enmeshment in close relationships, a need to control the behavior of others, compulsive behaviors, constricted emotions, low self-esteem, over-responsibility for others, and feelings of powerlessness.

Statement of the Problem
The codependency of a counselor can be of profound

importance to the client as well as to that therapist and any agency involved in the counseling process. This book includes not only an overall examination of codependency but also discusses how the therapist may fall into codependent styles of interaction. Codependent behaviors in the therapist are examined from several theoretical viewpoints. The effects of codependency on client-therapist relationships and possible methods of breaking these patterns of behavior are presented. While the topic is discussed primarily from the perspective of and in the language of the alcoholism/chemical dependency field, the problem of codependent behavior as it appears to be applicable to the field of therapy is examined.

Background

Clients use the therapeutic relationship as a model to learn new ways of establishing relationships or improving current ones. In a functional counseling relationship, the therapist and patient become more involved with each other as levels of trust increase. Regardless of therapeutic orientation, from psychoanalytic to person-centered, it is within the helping relationship that the client develops the skills needed for change (Brammer and Shostrom, 1982).

The client-counselor relationship is similar to any other relationship a person may have. Every person, whether client or therapist, uses those methods of establishing and maintaining relationships which have worked most effectively in the past. These methods are based on the individual values, attitudes, and beliefs that the person uses in daily life. Whether with family, friends, or even co-workers, all of an individual's relationships tend to follow the same general functional or dysfunctional patterns largely because of these experiences, values, beliefs, and attitudes.

*Both the client and the counselor
bring their own interpersonal
issues and histories into
the therapy relationship.*

This means that the same developmental issues of trust, intimacy, and respect which are found in non-therapeutic relationships are also found in the counseling situation. Ideally the counseling relationship works only with the client's own issues and none of the therapist's unresolved problems are brought into play. The reality is that the therapist may not always have control over whose issues come into the session. If the counselor's personal problems regularly are allowed to take precedence over the client's needs, a dysfunctional counseling relationship can result.

Counselor influence on the patient is stronger than many therapists wish to admit. The client's own values, attitudes, and beliefs about medical professionals and counselors in general have a strong impact on the relationship. This "medical model" frequently involves the concept of the professional doing something which cures or fixes the problem; the patient is a passive recipient of the treatment. These attitudes, values, and beliefs may block the client's progress in therapy. The more power a patient assumes the therapist to have, or the more infallible the counselor feels, the more chance that therapy will be ineffective. Codependent behavior by the therapist may tend to strongly support these client values, beliefs, and attitudes. This support also may work to prevent successful outcomes of therapy.

Significance to the Study

Counselors are responsible for the skills they possess,

how these skills are used, the types of interventions made, and for ethical behavior. The therapist who makes appropriate recommendations and provides adequate follow-up on those suggestions must then depend upon the client to use the interventions as intended. The client is the only one who can determine which interventions are used or ignored and how those interventions are applied. It is for this reason that Friedman (1985) states that the client bears much of the responsibility for the successful outcomes of therapy.

Regardless of theoretical orientation, therapists are susceptible to codependent attitudes and behaviors. A counselor who believes that he or she has the ability to transform a client into something or someone different or that he or she is responsible if the client chooses not to change is falling into the role of the "Professional Codependent."

The therapist who engages in codependent behaviors becomes a part of the alcoholic or problem system and reinforces denial—in fact, becomes an accomplice to the alcoholic/addict.

Furthermore, the counselor enters into a partnership with all the other codependents in the alcoholic's system to protect the drinker from experiencing the negative consequences of drinking behavior. When therapists fall into codependent behavior, the patient is subjected to lowered effectiveness and quality of therapy. At the same time the counselor suffers increased stress in the therapy session and in other relationships which may contribute to periods of burnout, depression, or substance abuse problems.

This book is presented with the intention of increasing therapist awareness of the problems of codependency in both personal and professional lives. By examining the problem from selected viewpoints the applicability of the concept is made clearer, and possible solutions become more apparent. It is believed that this increased awareness can have a significant impact on counselor effectiveness and self-esteem.

Definitions and Discussion

Before proceeding further, a few of the terms and concepts used in this book need to be defined. Some of the terms are used interchangeably and are presented as alternates for the same definition. For the purposes of this book, the following definitions are used:

Therapist/Counselor: Any individual who works in a therapeutic or counseling situation regardless of the title of the position. This includes licensed and unlicensed individuals as well as clergy, lay and paraprofessional workers.

Client/Patient: Any individual who seeks therapy or counseling from a therapist.

System: Any family or other group to which an individual belongs in which multiple, complex interpersonal relationships are the norm. The concept also includes work groups and treatment teams.

Codependency: Codependency is a potentially dysfunctional pattern of interpersonal behaviors and traits most often seen in those persons who are in relationships with chemically dependent or other dysfunctional people. These characteristics are seen primarily in their interactions within that relationship, but may extend to other relationships. Some of these include

* difficulty in forming/maintaining close relationships

- constricted emotions
- perfectionism
- a need to control the behavior of others
- compulsive behaviors
- feeling overly responsible for others
- feelings of powerlessness
- shame
- low self-esteem

Codependency is still in the process of being thoroughly defined. One of the definitions currently in use is as follows:

Codependency is a condition which can emerge from any family system where certain unwritten, even unspoken rules exist...a dysfunctional pattern of living and problem-solving which is nurtured by a set of rules within the family system. — Subby and Friel, 1984, p. 4

These rules are those which are common to many families and groups which are isolated and dysfunctional.

- "Don't tell anyone our problems."
- "Don't show what you feel."
- "Don't talk directly to someone else."

The preceding are some examples of the rules found in these dysfunctional systems. Other maxims heard in these systems are

- "Children should be seen and not heard."
- "Do as I say, not as I do."
- "Act your age."
- "Men don't cry."
- "If you can't say something nice, don't say anything at all." — Subby and Friel, 1984, p. 4

The common traits of all of these rules are non-negotiable rigidity and unidentified authority (everyone knows this rule is true but no one knows who made it, and since no one knows where the rule comes from, it is impossible to try to suggest modifications).

> *The ultimate rule in this system*
> *may be, "I know what the rules*
> *are and you have to guess;*
> *if you guess one then I'll change it."*

Susan, Nursing Director

I really hate this place. It just gets worse and worse. I feel like it is impossible to find any nurses who are willing to put up with the hassles of working in a chemical dependency unit and the ones I have are getting more and more unreliable. Furthermore, I have troubles with Tom because he says that my nurses cause all of the problems with the patients.

I just wish that things would settle down. It seems like I only just get all of the changes in place when something new comes along. The procedures which made sense and worked well seem to change for no reason or without apparent good effect. The rest of the changes have no effect because no one ever follows up on them and the patients continue in the old way.

I try to keep my nurses under control, but because they make so many mistakes, I have to do a lot of crisis management and make policy decisions on the spot. They never seem to understand what it is I have to do to keep this place running as smooth as it does. I even had to fire my best nurse the other day for insubordination after she got angry and told me that I was not consistent in my rules. She got even angrier when I told her that I treated my nurses on a case-by-case basis.

Cermak (1986b) defines codependency as

A recognizable pattern of personality traits, predictably found within most members of chemically dependent families, which are capable of creating sufficient dys-

36

DIAGNOSTIC CRITERIA FOR CODEPENDENT PERSONALITY DISORDER

A. Continued investment of self-esteem in the ability to control both oneself and others in the face of serious adverse consequences.

B. Assumption of responsibility for meeting others' needs to the exclusion of acknowledging one's own.

C. Anxiety and boundary distortions around intimacy and separation.

D. Enmeshment in relationships with personality disordered, chemically dependent, other codependent, and/or impulse disordered individuals.

E. Three or more of the following:
 1. Excessive reliance on denial
 2. Constriction of emotions (with or without dramatic outbursts)
 3. Depression
 4. Hypervigilance
 5. Compulsion
 6. Anxiety
 7. Substance abuse
 8. Has been (or is) the victim of recurrent physical or sexual abuse
 9. Stress-related medical illnesses
 10. Has remained in a primary relationship with an active substance abuser for at least two years without seeking help

Figure 1: From *Diagnosing and Treating Co-Dependence* by Timmen L. Cermak. See permissions, p. 4.

function to warrant the diagnosis of Mixed Personality Disorder as outlined in the DSM-III.—p. 1.

Certainly this definition seems to require much more stringent application as a diagnostic tool than does the definition provided by Subby and Friel. Cermak's diagnostic criteria are based on several clusters of symptoms characteristic of codependent individuals and are presented in DSM-III format for use in diagnosis and development of treatment plans (Figure 1).

Cermak provides additional guidelines and justification for his definition and diagnostic criteria. It is important for the person making the diagnosis to fully consider the implications of these criteria. Personality traits are the ways an individual perceives, relates to, and thinks about self and the environment and are displayed in many social and personal situations. These traits become a problem only when they are so inflexible and counterproductive as to cause loss of ability to function in social or occupational settings or cause major feelings of distress. The presence of these traits does not automatically carry a diagnosis of a personality disorder but instead should be seen as an indicator of possible problems. Cermak has presented these criteria in a format which is intended to bring the concept of codependency out of the isolation of the chemical dependency field and into the broader areas of therapy. These criteria, as modified to reflect codependent behaviors in counselors, are discussed here and some examples of therapist codependence are provided for additional clarity.

A. **Investment of self-esteem in patient change:** In order for a therapist to feel good about himself or herself, the patient must continually do well in therapy. A failure of the patient in treatment causes the counselor to doubt therapeutic skills and abilities with a subsequent loss of self-esteem. The fundamental belief that a counselor should have the ability to make a client change is a denial of the innate fallibility and powerlessness an individual always has in any relationship.

Sam, Inpatient Chemical Dependency Counselor

It's getting to the point that I hate to go to the staffing sessions. Our medical director and psychologist are really starting to get carried away with their need to put people into residential treatment. Some of the patients they want to put away have done really well in my treatment groups and I think that they don't pay enough attention to my opinion on the matter.

I can't see why they think that my patients are more resistant to treatment interventions than Mary's patients or even those of the other counselors. I work so hard with them and they all do so well.

Their criticism really hurts and I feel so resentful about this nonsense. If they think I am such a lousy counselor, why don't they just tell me instead of attacking my patients?

B. Assumption of responsibility for clients: To help the client, the therapist suppresses personal feelings, reactions, and needs in favor of those of the client in order to avoid angering the patient or to keep him or her happy. The therapist does not take a firm position with regard to last-minute cancellations, no-shows, incomplete therapeutic assignments, or failure to pay on time.

C. Anxiety and boundary distortions in the therapeutic relationship: As the counseling relationship develops and the counselor begins to establish emotional rapport with the client, that counselor may begin to experience confusion and anxiety and even a sense of loss of self. The continuously changing boundaries between the individuals involved presents the codependent counselor with the dilemma of having to differentiate between client and self when the tendency is to suppress self and join the client.

D. Enmeshment in relationships with clients: The codependent counselor does not confront the patient's denial, is tolerant of client projections, and accepts or even offers additional rationalizations to the client. The therapist mirrors those patient behaviors which are symptomatic of the problem. The codependent counselor and the client enter into a mutually gratifying relationship in which the client's behavior is never challenged.

E. Three or more of the following:

1. Excessive reliance on denial. The codependent therapist, when faced with the growing evidence of his or her own codependence, quickly points to those symptoms which are not present as proof that there is no problem. This, of course, allows that counselor to avoid the feelings associated with recognition and acceptance of a problem. It also allows that individual to avoid having to change.

2. Constriction of emotions. The codependent counselor will typically expend massive amounts of time and energy to avoid or restrict negative or "bad" feelings such as

- anger
- fear
- embarrassment
- inadequacy
- sadness
- loneliness

This repression of feelings also blocks access to all of the positive or "good" feelings which a person experiences. This can result in the therapist overreacting inappropriately to relatively minor events, often in relationships outside of the therapy relationship.

3. *Depression.* This usually will be denied since an admission of depression presents an unwanted focus on the personal feelings of the codependent therapist. This admission would mean that the therapist has needs which are being placed ahead of those of a client, and of course that is unacceptable behavior under criterion B.

4. *Hypervigilance.* Having invested self-esteem in the responses of the client, the therapist must remain extremely alert in order to ensure that the client remains happy and successful in therapy. Even the slightest sign of failure must be dealt with immediately to avoid subsequent undesired emotions.

5. *Compulsion.* The therapist whose self-esteem, feelings, dedication, and responsibility are invested in clients' success in treatment will experience unwanted feelings when the patient is not in compliance with the expectations of the counselor. The therapist may then attempt to avoid the negative feelings by a flurry of activity which is compulsive in nature. As long as the compulsion is in charge, the therapist does not have to experience the unwanted feelings.

6. *Anxiety.* As the therapist maintains denial of the nature of the relationship with the client, levels of anxiety increase and are taken as another sign of therapeutic inadequacy. This anxiety can be free-floating anxiety, chronic anxiety, or even existential dread. The threatened loss of self if the patient fails in therapy is seen as the source of the existential fears.

7. *Substance abuse.* Drug or alcohol use is a common response to stress and unwanted emotions in an apparent attempt to deny, avoid, or change the feelings. Therapists are not immune to this response, and as Cermak points out:

The codependent who compulsively uses chemicals in the service of denial is diagnosed as chemically dependent. This is as it should be; when chemical dependence is present, it must always be treated as the primary issue. But it cannot be seen as the only issue. *Once the chemical dependence has been broken, the codependence remains; left untreated, it acts as a barrier to long term sobriety.—Cermak, 1986a, pp. 29-30.*

8. *Victim of emotional abuse.* While physical or sexual abuse may not be present in the therapeutic relationship, the threat of physical violence may often be present. This may be felt in the abusive anger or threatening behavior of the patient in the session directed at someone in the client's life or even toward the therapist. It can also be found in the emotional responses of the counselor to this type of behavior. The therapist who leaves the office feeling "beat up" after a session has been subjected to emotional abuse. A pattern of denial of emotional states leads to denial of feeling abused and an inability on the part of the therapist to view the situation realistically. The inability to recognize the abusive nature of the relationship and terminate or change such a relationship is a symptom of therapist codependence.

9. *Stress-related medical illnesses:* Codependent relationships are extremely stressful. The therapist who is in one of these relationships routinely denies the stress or that the stress has any effect. Over time, chronic stress leads to such physical conditions as headaches, asthma, high blood pressure, stroke, rashes, and gastritis. Counselors who are codependent in their relationships with clients are equally subject to these physical problems as well as other symptoms of burnout.

10. *Remains in therapeutic relationship with an unchanging client:* A therapist who fails to seek outside assistance or consultation concerning a client who

never makes any progress is acting in a codependent manner. Cermak stated that if a chemically dependent/codependent relationship continues for two or more years without the non-chemically dependent member seeking outside help then a diagnosis of codependence must be considered. The same consideration must be made for a therapeutic relationship. However, if ethical treatment is to be considered, perhaps one year or less is more appropriate when talking about codependency in counselor/client relationships.

It is possible for a person to be in a codependent relationship without being actively involved with a chemically dependent person. It is also possible for the individual to develop codependent behavior patterns without ever having been in a relationship with a chemically dependent person (Subby and Friel, 1984).

The codependent uses these behaviors as "standard operating procedure" in almost all personal interactions. The extent the traits appear in any transaction is in large part a reaction to the behavior of the other person.

Gierymski and Williams (1986) believe that caution needs to be observed in defining codependency with a too specific terminology and diagnostic criteria.

Even if the behaviors, attitudes and emotion associated with this so-called disease are shared by many family members living with alcoholics, there is no convincing evidence that such a proposed constellation is not shared by many family members of other families with a chronic disease, such as schizophrenia, diabetes, Alzheimer's or mental retardation, in their various phases of development. —p. 12.

This supports the view that codependency may be broader in scope than what is implied by "co-alcoholism." Both Cermak (1986a, 1986b) and Subby and Friel (1984) agree that the chemcially dependent family is not the only source of problems with code-pendency.

ENABLING: One of several terms referring to specific behaviors which are typically codependent.

Enabling is simply any behavior on the part of any individual, whether family member, friend, co-worker, or even therapist, which makes it easier for the chemically dependent member to continue the addictive behavior.

An example is failure to confront a client on continued substance abuse when that drug use impacts on satisfactory outcomes of therapy. In the case of a therapist, this can be extended to include failure to confront a patient on any counterproductive pattern of behavior which affects resolution of the initial or subsequent problem. Institutions may also enable an individual to continue with negative behavior through the normal provision of services such as welfare, food stamps, medical care, and other similar services.

A therapist with codependent personality traits may be at extreme risk for entering into a codependent relationship with her or his clients. If this happens, significant and severe problems for the therapist, the client, and the agency can develop. The agency can develop the typical characteristics of a dysfunctional family. The codependent therapist becomes a part of the patient's problem system and may actually help aggravate the problem rather than helping solve it. Therapists may eventually experience periods of burnout and stress-related illness. There are some specific behaviors associated with codependency which can be problematic in

the therapeutic relationship. Codependent behaviors which cause problems in the counseling relationship are:
- Enabling
- Rescuing
- Persecuting
- Being victimized
- Need to control others
- Enmeshment in relationship with clients
- Restricted emotions
- Lack of assertiveness
- Inability to set limits with clients

and the other behaviors and attitudes listed by Cermak in Figure 1.

The appearance of these behaviors in a therapist signals the need for intervention on the part of co-workers, friends, supervisors, family, or even clients. This book will examine the potential extent of the problem of codependent counselors as well as some workable methods to be used by the individual therapist or supervisor to resolve the problem.

Chapter 2

Basic Theory/
Literature Review I

This literature review of basic theory will address the following six aspects of codependency:

- the alcoholism/chemical dependency field perspective
- family roles and codependency
- styles of enabling behavior
- children of alcoholics research
- codependency assessment research
- adult children of alcoholics

These aspects will provide the basis for further examination of the concept of codependency.

Alcoholism/Chemical Dependency Field
Perspective

Codependent behavior is part of the system which supports alcoholic or addictive behavior. Codependent behaviors reinforce the chemically dependent member's denial and allow the drug use to continue unabated. Denial is the sum of the unconscious suppression, repression, projection, and rationalization processes used by both the addict and the codependent to help them

47

believe that chemical dependency is not a problem and that life is normal.

Codependent members of the system behave as they do in order to cope with life in an addictive/abusive system. Codependents are frequently members of the alcoholic or addict's family but may also be friends, co-workers, or others who have a relationship with the addict. Early discussions of codependency frequently took the position that the behaviors were developed as a reaction to someone else's drug or alcohol dependency and were not a separate problem. While the development may have been as stated, a person can continue in the pattern of codependent behaviors even after that relationship no longer exists. Codependent behavior patterns can also be found in interactions outside that primary relationship. Codependent behaviors as listed by Cermak have been noted in members of families where physical or sexual abuse or some other dysfunctional behavior was present, but where no drug or alcohol abuse was noted.

Codependency can be diagnosed as a problem, even if any pre-existing or co-existing problem in another person cannot be identified in the current situation.
—Cermak, 1986a; Schaef, 1986; Wegscheider-Cruse, 1985.

One of the other terms which has been applied to the codependent is "enabler" which very simply means any individual, whether family member, friend, co-worker, or therapist, whose behavior can be classed as enabling. This, as discussed earlier, is any behavior which makes it easy or easier for the addict or problem family member to continue the addictive or problem behavior. The enabler actually denies the alcoholic the chance to assume responsibility for the consequences of negative behavior. The enabler assists in the alcoholic's cover-up (Levinson and Straussner, 1978) or in attempts to disguise problem behaviors and conditions.

Since codependent behavior tends to support the continued use of the drug of choice or continuation of the presenting problem, further examination of the concept as it applies to the therapeutic relationship is appropriate. The relationship between a client and therapist is recognized as essential to the success or failure of therapy. This relationship can be considered to be a helpful agent in its own right through the process of establishing a strong, positive, and mutual "working" relationship (Brammer and Shostrom, 1982). Dixon (1986) states that "'Enabling' is contrapositive and ruinous, and can, in no way ever be considered a loving, supporting, and helpful action" (p. 33).

Codependents develop denial about the need to feel in control of the world around them. Each time they find themselves unable to control the problem behavior of the addict or alcoholic, they assume a heavier burden of guilt and inadequacy.

As a result there is an expenditure of ever increasing amounts of time and energy in the attempt to gain control over the environment and the behavior of themselves and the alcoholic.

This concept can be expanded to cover the continued unsuccessful attempts of a family member to control any negative behavior of another family member.

Eventually a codependent comes to measure personal self-esteem by his or her ability to control the other person's behavior. When multiple attempts to control are unsuccessful, the enabler's self-esteem gets lower. As self-esteem gets progressively lower the codependent becomes more and more compulsive in the attempts to control the problem behavior. Frequently, the continued use of the drug or continuation of the acting out behavior is seen as visible proof of the enabler's failure and inadequacy.

Self-esteem seems inversely proportional to the problem behavior or chemical use; the more the behavior occurs, the lower the self-esteem.
—Cermak, 1986a; Johnson Institute, undated.

Tom M.

I just can't understand it. My reputation as a program director was really good a few months ago when the unit was doing well, and now I am looked down on by the other program directors. I think it is because our nursing staff just can't seem to get it together and no matter how hard I try, they just don't make it.

Of course, when the nursing staff makes more mistakes, the rest of the staff suffers as well and then their performance goes down. And that means that our competition hears about it and then we don't get referrals.

When the nurses and the counselors are working well, we are very successful and then we look really good. It just isn't fair that my reputation suffers at the hands of others.

Family Roles and Codependency

People living in a family with an addict, alcoholic, or some other type of dysfunctional person develop various methods of interaction with the other members of the family. These methods are roles or stereotyped behaviors and attitudes which allow the individual to survive in the family. Each member of the family takes on a different role which is determined by relative positions in the family. Taken together the roles in the family present a system often described as being as delicately balanced as a mobile (Wegscheider, 1981).

The roles are sometimes described as the Addict, Enabler, Hero, Scapegoat, Lost Child, and Mascot. Each role is seen as that individual's means of coping with and surviving the stresses of the alcoholic family. The Addict is the chemically dependent member of the family and that person's chemical use is the main identifying characteristic of this role. The Enabler is most often the spouse of the Addict and is easily identified by apparent powerlessness and self-righteousness while trying to control the behavior of the Addict. The Hero is most often the oldest child and is known as an overachiever. Delinquent behavior is the trademark of the Scapegoat. The Lost Child is rarely seen because of shyness and solitary behavior while the Mascot is always visible with his or her hyperactivity and clowning (Wegscheider, 1981). These roles make up the enabling system of a typical chemically dependent family according to one frequently used model.

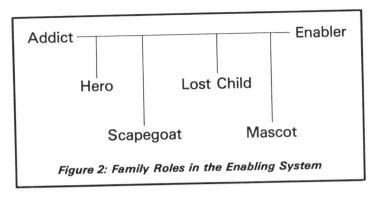

Figure 2: Family Roles in the Enabling System

During the childhood years, the parents give messages which frequently are critical. Such messages are internalized and result in low self-esteem or a negative self-image. Such children learn the following messages as a part of growing up: "Don't talk, don't trust, don't feel" (Black, 1981, p. 29). As these children learn to deny their personal feelings, they experience

something worse than "low self-esteem"! Such denial creates a feeling of having no self, of being hollow inside.... Denial creates feelings of confusion and of having to rely upon the reaction of others as a guide to action. Codependents constantly seek approval (Baasel, 1986 p. 25).

These children join the enabling system and cooperate with the primary enabler to help the addicted member maintain the drug habit.

As the feelings of inadequacy, self-doubt, guilt, and low self-esteem mount, the enabler continues to accept responsibility for the ongoing behavior of the addict and for the stress created by the chemical dependency. The enabler feels responsible for the addict's intoxication and/or recovery from the disease. While it is true that each member of a system contributes to the maintenance and operation of the system, the enabler does not realize that he or she is not the cause of the drinking or drug usage. Unfortunately, codependents also do not realize their powerlessness to stop chemical use by the alcoholic. Responsibility for changing the drinking or drug behavior always lies with the addict.

Styles of Enabling Behavior

Codependents behave the way they do in the sincere belief that what they are doing will help the situation and the addict.

Their denial prevents them from seeing that their own behavior makes things worse and not better.

Things other than the chemicals or the addict are blamed for the behavior of the addict. Stresses such as work problems, financial problems, family tension, and health or emotional problems are seen as the cause of the family's troubles. Codependents are confused by the increasing problems as things in their lives get worse despite their best efforts and intentions. What seems to happen is that the addict continues to use the drug and may increase that usage while pointing to the behavior of the codependent as the reason for use (Nelson, 1985).

Nelson (1985) discusses his studies of the enabling behavior of individuals who are codependent in a relationship with a cocaine addict. He has identified six broad categories of behavior which he labels "Styles of Enabling Behavior" (Figure 3) with respect to these codependents. His concepts can easily be extended to the entire range of codependency whether with alcoholics, addicts, or those individuals with other dysfunctional behaviors.

The following discussion of these styles of behavior will demonstrate how the concept of therapist codependency fits into these patterns of behavior. Examples of each type of enabling behavior specifically related to therapists have been included for additional clarity.

Styles of Enabling Behavior

1. *Avoiding and Shielding:* Any behavior by the codependent covering up for, or preventing the abuser, or self from experiencing the full impact of harmful consequences of drug use.
2. *Attempting to Control:* Any behavior by the codependent performed with the intent to take personal control over the significant other's drug use.
3. *Taking over Responsibilities:* Any behavior by the codependent designed to take over the abuser's personal responsibilities, such as household chores or employment.
4. *Rationalizing and Accepting:* Any behavior by the codependent conveying a rationalization or acceptance of the significant other's drug use.
5. *Cooperating and Collaborating:* Any assistance or involvement by the codependent in the buying, selling, adulterating, testing, preparing, or use of drugs.
6. *Rescuing and Subserving:* Any behavior by the codependent overprotecting the abuser and subjugating himself or herself.

Figure 3: From TREATING COCAINE DEPENDENCY by David E. Smith, M.D., and Donald R. Wesson, M.D., copyright 1988, by Hazelden Foundation, Center City, Minnesota. Reprinted by permission.

Avoiding and Shielding is any action by the therapist which covers up for or prevents the addict from experiencing the natural consequences of the negative behavior. For example, a counselor who fails to confront a client about a known or suspected drug problem is being codependent. Another example is a therapist who fails to include a diagnosed alcohol problem in the assessment of patient needs and development of treatment plans; such a failure is codependent behavior.

Attempting to Control is anything done by the counselor in attempting to take personal control over the patient's behavior. A codependent counselor is one who constantly reminds and nags the client to complete therapeutic assignments rather than confronting the failure as a therapeutic issue. The therapist who offers and withdraws treatment and services based on client behavior and compliance is attempting to control the patient.

Taking Over Responsibilities is any behavior by the therapist which effectively takes over the abuser's personal responsibilities. A therapist who routinely makes telephone calls and appointments for the client instead of requiring the client to assume responsibility for his or her own recovery is enabling the patient. The counselor who routinely calls to remind clients of scheduled appointments is also taking over responsibility for the patient's behavior.

Rationalizing and Accepting is any behavior by the counselor which expresses a rationalization or acceptance of the other's behavior. A counselor who accepts without question a client's excuses for failing to complete therapeutic assignments may be exhibiting this behavior. The therapist who makes such excuses for a client's behavior as, "It isnt't his fault he drinks; he has so many traumatic problems going on in his life," is acting in a codependent manner.

Cooperating and Collaborating is any involvement by the therapist in the buying and/or use of drugs or active participation in the patient's negative behavior. Any therapist or social worker who provides access to emergency or other funds knowing that the client will use the money for something other than the designated purpose is collaborating with the negative behavior. Another example is the counselor who helps a patient find new means of avoiding the consequences of behavior; i.e., helping to meet requirements for assistance programs when not truly qualified because of some behavior or failure at compliance on the part of the client.

Rescuing and Subserving is any action which overprotects the client and at the same time places the counselor under the control of the patient. A therapist who intervenes between a client and some authority whose intent is to enforce sanctions such as imprisonment and other punishment because of the client's behavior may be rescuing the client. A counselor who, when the client does not comply with the requirements of the treatment program, fails to apply the consequences required by policies and procedures of the program again is saving the patient from the natural consequences of the negative behavior.

Codependents need to receive treatment for codependency concurrently with the addict. Treatment should attempt to identify those styles of enabling, as listed in Figure 3, which are the primary and secondary modes the codependent uses. (Appendix 3 is a questionnaire based on the styles of enabling behavior for use in identifying these issues with clients.) Once identified, alternatives for each of these types of behavior need to be developed through appropriate counseling and education processes (Nelson, 1985).

Therapist Styles of Enabling Behavior Checklist

Ask yourself about each of the behaviors listed under each style of behavior. The one or two styles with the most positive responses are the styles which need to be included in the treatment planning and education processes.

1. Avoiding and Shielding: Have you ever...?
   ____Made up excuses for your patients
   ____Ignored evidence of drug use by clients
   ____Threatened to terminate a client from treatment
   ____Shielded patient from crisis
   ____Helped client keep appearances up
   ____Covered up for patient with family or employer

2. Attempting to Control: Have you ever...?
   ____Stayed home from work to avoid client's problems
   ____Constantly reminded/preached about patient's failures
   ____Screamed, yelled, swore, cried trying to force quitting
   ____Stayed away from work to get away from it all
   ____Told patient to leave, then went looking for patient
   ____Offered/withdrawn services based on client behavior

3. Taking over Responsibilities: Have you ever...?
   ____Always made sure patient was on time for appointments
   ____Made telephone calls for clients

4. Rationalizing and Accepting: Have you ever...?
   ____Accepted excuses for failure to complete assignments
   ____Made excuses for patient-continued drug use
   ____Made excuses for self-defeating behavior of the client
   ____Accepted patient's excuses for drug use

5. Cooperating and Collaborating: Have you ever...?
   ____Helped client get money from emergency funds
   ____Helped patient avoid consequences of behavior
   ____Loaned patient money

6. Rescuing and Subserving: Have you ever...?
   ____Intervened for patient with probation or other authority
   ____Not applied consequences for failure at treatment

Family counseling is recognized as a necessary adjunct to, but not a replacement for, treatment for addiction, but this need is frequently expressed in terms indicating that the family's treatment and recovery from each member's codependency issues is secondary to and supportive of the addict's needs. Many treatment programs/counseling agencies still do not recognize codependency as a problem for family members who are not primary addicts; nor do they provide treatment for them regardless of whether or not the addict receives treatment.

Many people who go into the helping professions come from exactly the family background described in the previous section.

Many therapists come from an
alcoholic home or other dysfunctional
family system in which they
learned codependent behavior.
— Cermak, 1986a; Wegscheider, 1982.

When people grow up trying to help or fix their family, they frequently take those helping/fixing behaviors and attitudes into their adult relationships, including the client-therapist relationship. It is therefore quite possible for such counselors to display codependent behavior with respect to a client.

When the therapist assigns blame for the situation to the spouse of the addict, the counselor is enabling the addict's behavior. Staff members of treatment programs who are not adequately trained in codependency may frequently address the codependent as the cause of the addiction and relapse. Such professionals are exhibiting (1) *Rationalizing and Accepting* and (2) *Avoiding and Shielding* as styles of codependent behavior in their own interactions with addicted clients. At the same time, codependent behaviors of blaming and attempting to control are present in the counselor's relationship with the other members of the client's system.

Perhaps agencies and treatment facilities hiring therapists need to consider screening prospective employees for codependency as part of the employment process. This could be done using a simple questionnaire designed to identify potential problem areas. A sample questionnaire is presented here.

Therapist Codependency Screening Interview

	Yes	No
1. I think that it is important to help the client at all costs.	_____	_____
2. I don't want to embarrass my clients, so I don't pry into their drinking habits.	_____	_____
3. It is important to protect my clients from any negative labels; I don't enter alcoholism into my treatment plans so the insurance companies won't punish them for being alcoholic.	_____	_____

---

4. If my clients do not complete my assignments, I think that they had more important things to do. _____ _____

5. If my client does not follow my directions, I punish him or her by reducing services or even terminating him/her from treatment. _____ _____

6. I try not to trouble my clients by requiring them to make calls to specialists because I can do it myself and make sure it is done right. _____ _____

7. I always call my clients the afternoon before their next appointment so they don't miss it. _____ _____

8. I don't want my clients to think I am angry, so I just accept whatever excuse they offer for not completing my assignments. _____ _____

9. I understand my client's problems and when I am talking with my peers, I do not hesitate to point out all of the things that contribute to the problem so that they understand that my clients are not fully responsible. _____ _____

10. Helping my client is more important than following all of the rules which are just intended to slow things down. _____ _____

11. Sometimes it is necessary to protect my client from the authorities in order to provide help. _____ _____

12. I know that my clients do not intentionally disregard the rules of the program where I work, so I rarely apply the required consequences for the violations. _____ _____

All questions are written in such a manner that a YES answer is a codependent response. This simple instrument is not intended to be diagnostic, but should be used in conjunction with the rest of an employment interview. Other similar questionnaires could be easily developed for other applications.

Children of Alcoholics Research

The actual number of codependents in the general population or in non-helping professions is not specifically available. Conservative estimates place the number of American children living in homes where alcohol is a problem at 20 million (DiCicco, 1981). Rogers (1978) states that up to one child in four in American schools comes from a home where alcohol is a problem. Seixas and Youcha (1985) estimate that there are at least 22 million adults in this country who grew up in homes with an alcoholic parent.

Gallup Polls in 1980 reported that 25 percent of Americans felt that alcohol-related problems had seriously affected their family; in 1982 that response had risen to 33% (National Institute on Alcohol Abuse and Alcoholism [NIAAA], 1980, 1982), while the 1986 survey reported the results of the same question as 21 percent (Gallup, 1986).

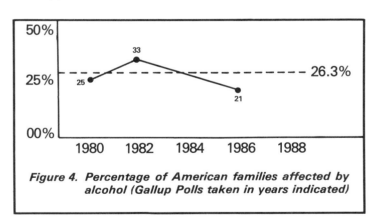

Figure 4. Percentage of American families affected by alcohol (Gallup Polls taken in years indicated)

The average of these three Gallup Polls is 26.3 percent; at present that figure will be assumed as representative of the number of individuals coming from homes where alcohol presented a problem. By the definition of codependency presented, this means that 26 percent may be taken as the lowest possible percentage of potential codependents in the general population.

Anecdotal data indicate that many individuals from this type of background go into the helping professions (Wegscheider, 1982; Cermak, 1986a). The question still remains as to whether or not a body of empirical evidence exists to support this anecdotal position. The first indications that this belief may be true come in the report by Policinski (1986) stating that an informal study of nursing trainees at the Memorial Hospital School of Nursing of South Bend, Indiana, found that up to 35 percent of the trainees in that program come from homes and marriages with at least one addict.

The Children of Alcoholics Screening Test (CAST) (Appendix 1) is a measure designed to identify individuals who are living with or have lived with an alcoholic. The test was administered to a group of children of alcoholics (n = 97) and a control group (n = 118). A cutoff of 6 points was established as the lowest score which included 100 percent of the children of alcoholics group. Using this cutoff as an indicator of being the child of an alcoholic, 23 percent of the control group were found to come from alcoholic homes (Pilat and Jones, 1985). This 23 percent correlates well with the general results of the Gallup surveys and the estimates quoted earlier.

Pilat and Jones (1985) also reported the administration of the CAST to a group of experienced therapists (n = 81), a group of social work and therapist students (n = 47), and a group of miscellaneous health professionals (n = 26). More than 28 percent of the experienced therapists, 25 percent of the students, and 46 percent of the miscellaneous professionals scored at least 6 points which identified them as children of alcoholics. This test also has a cutoff score at the 2+ point level which the author states indicates that the individual came from a home where abusive rather than alcoholic drinking caused problems (Jones, 1983). In the study of therapists, 36 percent of the students, 47 percent of the experienced therapists, and 54 percent of the miscellaneous professionals met this criteria.

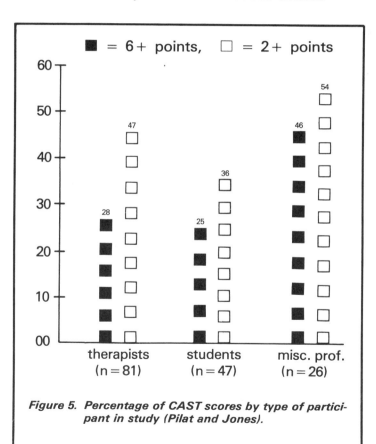

Figure 5. *Percentage of CAST scores by type of participant in study (Pilat and Jones).*

Assuming that the 26 percent reported by Gallup accurately estimates the proportion for the general population, Pilat and Jones's results indicate that there may be between 30 percent and 200 percent more children of alcoholics in the helping professions than there are in the same size sample of the general population. This tends to support the assertions of Wegscheider and Cermak that a significant number of children of alcoholics choose one of the helping professions as a career.

Codependency Assessment Research

Friel (1985) has published a preliminary Codependency Assessment Inventory (Appendix 2) as part of an attempt to develop a valid evaluation instrument to identify codependents. The inventory is a 60-item True-False test which attempts to cover such areas as
- self-care
- self-criticism
- secrets
- "stuck-ness"
- boundary issues
- family of origin
- feelings indentification
- intimacy
- physical health
- autonomy
- over-responsibility
- burnout
- identity

The scale used to score this assessment questionnaire has the potential to identify differing degrees of codependent issues. The scale is
- 20 or below = few codependent concerns
- 21-30 = mild/moderate codependent concerns

- 31-45 = moderate/severe concerns
- 45+ = severe.

Results of studies using this inventory have not yet been published, but Friel (personal communication, October 1, 1987) states that the inventory has been informally given to several groups of therapists, social workers, and health care professionals at seminars. Scores for these counselors have been quite high, ranging from 25 to 55, with mean group scores ranging from 30 to 40.

Friel (personal communication, October 1, 1987) also states that when using the inventory with clients in chemical dependency treatment programs average scores are in the area of 30-35 points. He states that counselors working on their own personal codependency issues score in the same average range. He did not indicate what percentage of counselors or clients scored below 20 or above 45 points.

Adult Children of Alcoholics

Woititz (1983) has identified thirteen behavior characteristics which she labels as typical of those of adult children of alcoholics. She states that the characteristics are consistently identified and generalized at group meetings by the individuals who attend. The specific meetings were those she held in her research work with Adult Children of Alcoholics. Since publication, these characteristics have been adopted by various Al-Anon or similar groups which have chosen to focus on the specific parent-child relationship in an alcoholic family rather than the more common spousal/partner relationship.

Because so many children of alcoholics seem to enter the helping professions, it becomes important for supervisors and other professionals to know the characteristics of those individuals. A therapist with the characteristics listed in the table which follows is at considerable risk of entering into an unhealthy relationship with a client who exhibits the appropriate triggering behaviors. A counselor's training will possibly have provided the opportunity to examine and work on many of these issues, but the nature of denial allows the individual to avoid seeing and dealing with issues. Counselors and supervisors need to be aware of the potential for disruptive behaviors from peers with this background.

Each category of traits offers specific problems for the therapist who is an adult child of an alcoholic. Each group contributes to the development of codependency in the therapist and each can contribute to specific problems in the therapeutic relationship. The counselor with the self-confidence characteristics listed may spend time seeking compliments from colleagues and patients as well as needing patients to always be successful in treatment. The relationship traits may interfere with the development of a suitable and appropriate client-counselor relationship with a resultant deterioration of the quality of therapy. Finally, the stress responses could be very destructive to established relationships with clients and co-workers and can also contribute to the incidence of burnout in the staff.

Adult Children of Alcoholics...

Self-confidence characteristics

- have difficulty completing what they start
- are merciless judges of themselves
- are extremely serious about themselves
- look for approval and recognition
- rarely allow themselves to have fun

Relationship characteristics

- remain loyal even when loyalty is undeserved
- have difficulty forming and maintaining close relationships
- are never sure what is normal behavior
- are extremely responsible or irresponsible
- feel somehow different from others

Stress response characteristics

- tell unnecessary lies when truth would serve
- tend to overreact to changes when they are powerless over the situation
- tend to be impulsive without considering alternatives or consequences leading to loss of self-esteem and feelings of loss of control

Figure 6: Characteristics of Adult Children of Alcoholics

Chapter 3

Alternate Theoretical Views/Literature Review II

An examination of different theories of personality development and therapy reveals that each has concepts which can explain the occurrence of codependent behavior patterns in the therapist. As various other theories are examined, concepts may be found which are compatible with codependency. The following theoretical perspectives are discussed in this chapter and have been chosen because of their common usage or particular relevance:

- Transactional Analysis
- Jungian theories
- Psychodynamics
- Family systems theory
- A multi-perspective viewpoint

Transactional Analysis

Interpersonal "games" of life and individual reactions to these games are among the basic ideas of Transactional Analysis (TA). Every "game" has definite rules, roles, and players. Games serve the function of allowing a person to interact with other people without the risk of intimacy while retaining the feeling of receiving some positive rewards from those same relationships. One set of games involves as "players" the alcoholic/addict and those persons who interact with that individual (Steiner, 1971).

Practitioners of Transactional Analysis do not write or speak of codependent behavior as such. There is, however, a concept in TA which corresponds to and describes the behavior patterns found in codependency. Steiner (1979) talks of some of the typical game roles or transactions found in alcoholic relationships.

The specific roles in the game are the three points of the Drama Triangle (Figure 7). In this triangle, the three roles are the Rescuer, the Persecutor, and the Victim. These are simplifications of the actual roles of real life, except in a game they also are dramatizations; therefore, these games are metaphors for the interpersonal transactions of daily living. We see ourselves as the virtuous Rescuers of Victims who may or may not appreciate our efforts, as righteous Persecutors of those who are wicked, and Victims of the terrible Persecutors. When playing any of these roles, it is easy to lose perspective of the realities that confront us.

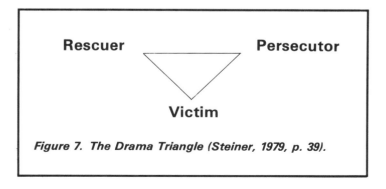

Figure 7. The Drama Triangle (Steiner, 1979, p. 39).

In the Drama Triangle the roles are arranged to show the relationship and the interchangeability of all three. An individual playing any one of the roles may change at any time to either of the other two positions. To the observer on the outside of the game, it is soon obvious that the Victim is not really as helpless as he or she appears to feel and act, that the Persecutor is playing out a complaint which frequently is not valid, and that the Rescuer does not really protect the Victim from anything or anyone.

Some of the alcoholic variations of the game described by Steiner (1971) are entitled

- "Drunk and Proud"
- "Lush"
- "Wino"

"Drunk and Proud" is described as a three-way game involving two persons. One is the alcoholic and the other player alternates between being the Victim and the Persecutor. The non-alcoholic partner is frequently the parent or spouse of the alcoholic who regularly faces the dilemma of choosing to accept the alcoholic's apologies and new promises for change or to act in a punitive fashion. This pattern of having to choose between being controlling and punishing or being passive and accepting is one of the major characteristics of co-dependency.

"Lush" is seen most often in female alcoholics. This is another three-way game which involves the alcoholic, a Rescuer, and a Victim. Again the Rescuer and Victim are interchangeable roles and are often played by the same person. These supporting scripts provide the alcoholic the means of or motivation for continuing the game. Frequently this game also involves a professional helper who assumes either of the non-alcoholic roles. The Rescuer and Victim in this game are very obviously enablers whose codependence is essential to the maintenance of the game.

In "Wino" everybody serves to help the alcoholic continue drinking by doing things which permit the game to continue. This game involves the alcoholic drinking so much that physical impairment occurs. Hospitalization and detoxification dry the alcoholic out enough to permit a return to drinking. Social workers, family, friends, hospitals, and even law enforcement personnel fill the Rescuer and Persecutor roles for the "Wino" game player. Almost any transaction this alcoholic game player has with another person can result in the continuation of drinking (Steiner 1971). Once again these behaviors of the nonalcoholic participants in the game are codependent in their patterns of enabling and controlling.

All of the nonalcoholic roles in the games "Drunk and Proud," "Lush," and "Wino" have typical behaviors as discussed. These behaviors fit easily into the definitions and models of codependency. The Drama Triangle effectively demonstrates the varying and circular patterns of behavior routinely seen in codependent systems.

The Drama Triangle and the Therapist:

Alcoholism can be viewed metaphorically as a game in a life-script. In order to help the alcoholic or addict, it is necessary for the therapist to remain clear of the game which is not always easily done. To remain clear of the game, the counselor must refuse to play any of the roles and instead must focus on the actual drinking or other self-defeating behavior of the patient.

> *Slipping into the role of Rescuer is so easy for the counselor that the concept must be of concern to anyone involved in helping others.*

The role of the Rescuer who attempts to help solve the problem for the alcoholic is frequently played by therapists. These counselors may actually defend the alcoholic against the "Persecutors" in the client's life as well as providing needed emotional support while the persecution is taking place. These Persecutors are often the spouse or employer of the alcoholic although it is not unusual for the alcoholic to present the judicial system as Persecutor.

Once the therapist discovers that the client is not responding to therapy and is in fact still drinking, a switch to the role of the Persecutor is not uncommon. The alcoholic may then be punished by a refusal to provide further treatment or by nagging and threatening to terminate treatment if the negative behavior does not change (Steiner, 1971).

Often the therapist who is unable to disengage from the game will feel resentment toward the alcoholic. Such counselors wonder why the alcoholic is "doing these things to them" and may start to doubt their own diagnostic and therapeutic skills. They begin to feel inadequate and depressed about all the things the alcoholic is "doing to them." In short, the therapist now assumes the Victim role in the game and sees the alcoholic as the Persecutor.

> *The counselor may fall into the same three roles of the alcoholic game as easily as the people in the alcoholic's circle of friends and family.*

Those who play the Rescuer role honestly believe that they are really helping the alcoholics and, of course, the alcoholics truly feel that they are the Victims. When either of them becomes a Persecutor, they believe that their complaint is valid and that their anger and behavior are completely justified.

Mary, Outpatient Chemical Dependency Counselor

This job is really so hard; lately it seems as if everyone has been getting on my case. Tom is always watching over my shoulder to see what I am doing with the clients, Sam is always digging at me because I have been sick, and even some of my patients have not been doing what I need to have them doing for their recoveries.

It used to be that everything here was really great. I was able to help my clients get into recovery, getting them past the most difficult problems against all odds, including legal problems. The nurses used to think that I was wonderful and that I could be counted on to help them any time they asked.

That changed after I lost my temper one day at a client who had smoked marijuana a couple of times after all I had done for him. I really chewed him out and nearly terminated him from treatment. As a matter of fact, what I did instead was to force him to pay his back bill, sign a new therapeutic contract which was much stricter, and finally to insist that he come to treatment meetings more frequently. I felt that this was totally appropriate as a therapeutic intervention, but apparently Tom, Sam, Susan, and everybody else thinks otherwise.

If they really cared about me, they would understand what it means to have a client do something like that to me and therefore they would understand why I had to act the way I did. Maybe it is time for me to look for another job.

While TA is not the primary orientation of most workers in the field of alcoholism and chemical dependency, the application of the Drama Triangle to codependency at once clarifies that concept and suggests a wider range of possible therapeutic interventions for working with codependents. It is possible to substitute any problem behavior in place of alcoholism or chemical dependency as the presenting problem for the system. On examination, all of the roles discussed for the game of alcoholism and the Drama Triangle will be found to hold true for other problems. With few exceptions, any individual with a diagnosis from the DSM-III-R is better able to sustain the problem behavior with a support system which is willing to tolerate, accept, and even encourage the problem.

Jungian Perspectives

Therapeutic Shadows:

Jungian theory and therapy do not specifically address the problem of alcoholism and the concept of the codependent relationship, but some of the constructs of Jungian theory do correspond with the concept. The therapist who is concerned about the problem of codependent behavior needs to pay attention to the Jungian concept of the Shadow.

The shadow side of an individual
is that part of the personality
which is unknown to that person,
but which affects personal behavior.

Some of the negative consequences an individual experiences in life are a result of the shadow side of the personality.

Many therapists and other health professionals appear to themselves and to others as being concerned about the well-being of mankind. A sincere desire to help others seems their prime motivation. Buried away in their unconscious, these individuals also have an equally large lust for power and joy, not in helping but in hindering clients. According to Jungian theory, when one has the purest and noblest of motives, the exact opposites appear somewhere in or near the individual (Guggenbuhl-Craig, 1971).

As the therapist enters into the relationship with the client, the shadow also enters. When the therapist is required to do something against the will of the client these shadow-side motivations come out. This type of power struggle, based on the highest ethical and moral standards, entices the counselor's darker aspect into being. The constellation of shadow aspects is the opposite of the visible aspects of the helping professional.

The therapist combines the visible components of two helping professions which are very powerful in the public eye—the doctor/healer and the priesthood.

But just as the doctor has the shadow aspect of the charlatan/quack and the priesthood carries the shadow of the false prophet, the therapist has the burden of both the charlatan/quack and the false prophet as Shadow (Guggenbuhl-Craig, 1971).

The dark side of the patient is the natural ally of both the charlatan and the false prophet, and the client can be expected to unconsciously encourage shadow-side behaviors on the part of the therapist. This alliance functions to prevent the counselor's awareness of the destructive activities in the therapeutic session. This unwillingness or inability of both the therapist and the patient to see shadow activity results in a shock to the counselor when the presence of unconscious operation is recognized.

One of Jung's premises was that whenever positive psychic energy appears in the conscious, the exact opposite is constellated in the unconscious. This opposite works against the good from that hidden position. Guggenbuhl-Craig (1971) says,

The physician becomes a charlatan precisely because he wants to heal as many people as possible; the clergyman becomes a hypocrite and false prophet precisely because he wants to bring people to the true faith, and the psychotherapist becomes an unconscious charlatan and false prophet although he works day and night on becoming more conscious.—pp. 31-32.

The stronger the therapist's desire to help as many people as possible, the stronger the pull of the shadow in the opposite direction.

The concept of the shadow becomes of obvious importance when applied to the dependent/codependent relationship. The more the codependent tries to help the dependent member of the relationship, the more that enabler feels resentful, guilty, and inadequate. The more the dependent member tries to control the substance abuse or problem behavior and fails, the more the feelings of guilt, inadequacy, and anger surface in that person. When the person with the codependent behavior is the therapist, the concept becomes even more significant. The negative feelings stirred in response to the client's behaviors and attitudes and the therapist behaviors resulting from those feelings constellate the shadow side of the desire to help.

Sometimes it seems as if clients seek a savior in the role of their therapist.

These clients hope to receive those secrets which will allow them to magically solve all of life's problems.

Guggenbuhl-Craig (1971) likens the beginning therapeutic relationship to "that of the sorcerer and his apprentice" (p. 38). The client's relationship fantasies about the therapist bring out the unconcious magician in the counselor. The therapist may begin to act as if the magical power to cure the client's problems truly exists.

The client's shadow works with the dark side of the therapist to sabotage treatment and the treatment relationship through resistance to therapy and change. This resistance and the charlatan work together naturally and sometimes appear to be symbiotic entities. The client's shadow believes in and works to empower the charlatan.

There is a part of the therapist
that wants to be completely in charge
of all aspects of the patient's life and
soul and that is the part which
cooperates with the client's shadow.
— *Guggenbuhl-Craig, 1971.*

The action of the shadow may appear in many highly unexpected ways. When the therapist needs to confront the client with difficult things, the shadow can appear. The therapist may use such a confrontation as a form of punishment to torment the client and to demonstrate power in the relationship. Another possibility is that the therapist will attempt to avoid conflict and will translate the unpleasantness of the confrontation into flattery. This flattery misleads clients into believing that they are doing well and that they are pleasing the therapist. Flattery begets flattery and soon the relationship becomes a mutual pact of building each other's feelings of self-worth. Therapy becomes a charlatan's confidence game in which both parties try to outdo the other and in which there are no winners.

The invariable alliance between the client's destructive aspect/shadow and the therapist's charlatan shadow is difficult for the therapist to block. Therapists who are willing to continuously and consistently confront and disclose their own dark side are more effective at helping clients confront shadow phenomena (Guggenbuhl-Craig, 1971).

Therapeutic Archetypes:

Jungian theory talks of archetypes and their effects on individual awareness and behaviors.

An archetype may be defined as an inborn potentiality of behavior. Human beings react archetypally to someone or something when faced with a typical, constantly recurring situation.... — Guggenbuhl-Craig, 1971, p. 89.

Archetypes are also seen as containing dual and opposite polarities, e.g., light and dark. Each human being seems to contain both poles at birth. If at any point one pole of the archetype is configured in the outside world, the inner and opposite pole is present nearby as well.

There does not seem to be either a specific healer or patient archetype. Instead, the healer and the patient are different poles of the same archetype. The healer-patient archetype appears when the individual gets sick. The healer aspect of the archetype is the "inner-healer" or the "will" to get better that is needed if a person is to recover from any illness. Vaillant (1983) states that the type of alcoholism treatment provided to a patient is not as important to recovery from the disease as the patient's ability to access the natural healing processes.

There is another variation of the healer-patient archetype which is encountered in many members of the healing professions. This is the "wounded healer" whose image appears consistently in the mythology of many cultures. This archetype means that the patient has a healer inside but, more important, that the counselor has a patient inside.

The internalized patient brings an awareness to the therapist that what is seen in the client is also within the counselor.
— *Guggenbuhl-Craig, 1971.*

This is frequently stated in the expression, "There but for the grace of God go I." Sandor (1987) expresses this when he says:

That was early on in my work with alcoholics and addicts—when I thought that I was fundamentally different from "them." After all, they were the patients and I was the doctor. Gratefully, some six years later, I have begun to learn otherwise. — p. 23.

It would seem that most members of the helping professions are subject to shadow problems. The desire to help mankind and the corresponding preoccupation with misfortune, social maladjustment, ignorance, and illness allow the shadow to become ever more powerful. The more aware and conscious the therapist becomes, the stronger the dark side's effect on the unconscious. It is difficult for anyone to know his or her own archetypal shadow of self-destructive behavior and tendencies. If Jung's premise is correct, it would seem that a therapist must be even more aware of the therapeutic shadow because of the potential for the simultaneous appearance of the shadow in clients.

While the concepts of the shadow, the archetype, and the archetypal shadow do not directly reflect the problems of codependency, the mutual interplay of the client-therapist shadow-sides directly parallels the dependent/codependent relationship. In the counselor, these unseen interactions are the behaviors of the codependent.

Psychodynamic Countertransference Phenomena

The psychoanalytically based concepts of transference and countertransference also contain the elements of a codependent relationship. The feelings and behaviors of the therapist toward a client frequently can directly correspond to those of the codependent.

Countertransference seems to be difficult to precisely define, but frequently expressed definitions in the literature range from the simple definition advanced by Stillson (1986) that "countertransference refers to the feelings induced in us by patients" (p. 21), to Imhof, Hirsch, and Terenzi (1983):

Countertransference is conceptualized as the total emotional reaction of the therapist to the patient, with consideration of the entire range of conscious, preconscious and unconscious attitudes, beliefs, and feelings in the therapist who comes in contact with a psychiatric patient who is also a drug abuser. — p. 492.

And to Brammer and Shostrum (1982), who state:

We view countertransference broadly to include conscious and unconscious attitudes of the counselor toward real or imagined client attitudes or overt behavior. — p. 227.

However, this book will use Davidson's (1977) definition:

Countertransference . . . will refer to the totality of the therapist's response to the patient. It includes reality factors such as the setting and working alliance with the patient, plus the internal responses of the therapist to the patient. — p. 121.

Even these definitions carry a resemblance to the definitions of codependency. The theories of codependency which see it as a reaction to the behavior of the addict could very easily be stated in terms of countertransference and transference.

Therapist Responses to Alcoholics:

Davidson (1977), Imhof, *et al.* (1983), and Wurmser (1974) have noted in the course of their work with addicts and alcoholics that most of these patients present a cluster of symptoms consistent with a psychiatric diagnosis of narcissistic and/or borderline personality disorders. Chemically dependent patients have been noted to consistently use the defense mechanisms most commonly found in these two personality types, specifically splitting and projective identification.

Many therapists have extreme difficulty keeping their objectivity and impartiality with respect to an alcoholic patient even though they may be able to maintain that same attitude with the most difficult non-alcoholic patient. When faced with an alcoholic, these therapists may become openly angry and impatient (Moore, 1961). Imhof *et al.* (1983) indicate that the therapist may be overwhelmed by the intense nature of the initial transference of the patient. They state that therapists frequently experience immediate hateful feelings toward the alcoholic patient. This is amplified by the therapeutic attitude that a therapist should not have negative feelings about a client.

Stillson (1986) takes the position that therapists can develop the behavioral characteristics of an alcoholic including

- impulsive behavior
- feelings of helplessness

- hopelessness
- cynicism
- powerlessness to control patient
- anger
- feelings of emptiness
- resentment
- boredom
- fatigue
- low tolerance for frustration, and
- emotional detachment

in response to working with their clients, almost as if the problem had been "caught" from the client. The similarity of these symptoms to those of burnout cannot be overlooked; in fact, Stillson sees a strong relationship between burnout and countertransference. She states that if the therapist is unable to recognize the countertransference and to turn the negative energy around to help the clients, that counselor will become burned out.

Chemically dependent patients frequently test and antagonize the therapist in an attempt to provoke punishment and scorn which strengthens the patient's attitude that "no one can ever be trusted" (Wurmser, 1978, p. 471). Davidson (1977) reports that patients who express strong emotions such as anger and blamefulness and who are openly hostile arouse equally strong reactions in the staff of a treatment agency or in the therapist providing treatment. Frequently these strong reactions take the form of punitive actions with the ultimate punishment being termination from treatment. Lesser sanctions may include more rigid enforcement of agency rules or more elaborate rules placing additional constraints on the client. This is done with the assumption or hope that the client will become more compliant and amenable to the agency's program. This form of interaction between patient and therapist can potentially develop into a codependent cycle of counselor confrontation and client acting out; the harsher the confrontation, the more severe the acting out becomes.

Therapist Roles:

Other reactions to client behaviors which may be seen in the therapist or clinical staff may be equally destructive of the benefits of therapy. Imhof *et al.* (1983, p. 503) describe the role of the "good parent rescuing the bad impulsive child." This therapist develops an enmeshed relationship with the client in which there is overinvolvement, overprotectiveness, permissive, and even maternal behavior as a demonstration of the therapist's love and goodness. There is a concurrent hope that this will prove to be the curative agent for the client. These feelings of a need to "save" or "rescue" the client are a denial of the fact that the therapist cannot control the client's decisions to continue drinking/using drugs or the decision to quit. If the therapist is unable to recognize feeling a need to control the client's behavior as a form of countertransference, the therapist may start to feel resentful, angry, bored, tired, helpless, and emotionally detached.

Another variation of the role a therapist may take is what Imhof *et al.* (1983, p. 504) labeled "you and me against the unjust world." When the therapist identifies with the client's anti-authoritarian life position or somewhat idealistically and romantically glamorizes the substance abuser's lifestyle, this role may appear. They state that such a position may stem from unresolved conscious and unconscious fantasies which are fulfilled vicariously when the client acts-out. The therapist may then be seen by the client as approving self-defeating behavior which then encourages the client to increase the behavior.

Therapist Roles as Countertransference

- **"Good parent rescuing the bad, impulsive child"**

    - overprotective
    - permissive
    - overinvolved
    - maternal
    - enmeshed

- **"You and me against the world"**

    - identifies with client's life position
    - glamorizes lifestyle
    - approving self-defeating behavior by client
    - vicariously living out fantasies

- **"Partners"**

    - avoid negative feelings
    - alliance with patient
    - rescue from other staff
    - protect against confrontations

- **"Chameleon"**

    - use reaction-formation as defense
    - attitude opposite to feelings
    - excessive indulgence and patience
    - agree with client that the "world is against him/her"

Figure 8: Therapist Roles as Countertransference

Davidson (1977) described another way a therapist may fall into this behavior. She said that patients may pair with a staff member, establishing a relationship in which negative feelings are avoided. Negative emotions are expressed toward other staff members in the form of dislikes and/or refusal to cooperate. This relationship is developed into an "alliance" against the rest of the staff; the therapist may rescue the patient from confrontations with other staff members. These rescues enable the patient to continue old behaviors and to sabotage the therapy.

Moore (1961) believes that many professionals who work with addicted/alcoholic clients use reaction formation as a defense mechanism to avoid the negative feelings of countertransference. In reaction formation, of course, the therapist adopts an attitude opposite to that actually felt. Instead of recognizing and allowing the feelings of anger and disgust at the alcoholic's behavior, the counselor may become excessively indulgent and patient. This therapist may develop such an attitude that any client request or demand is immediately granted. This attitude may be so strong that the therapist agrees with the view of the client that everyone is against him or her. Such an attitude corresponds directly with some of the common forms of denial found in chemically dependent and codependent individuals. This attitude does not help the client into recovery; it becomes an extension of the alcoholic denial system and once again the client is protected from experiencing the consequences of the addiction.

Countertransference or Codependency:

These examples of countertransference easily fit into the model of codependency presented. The attitudes and behaviors which are the therapist's reactions to the client's behavior are characteristic of codependence as well as fitting the model of Adult Children of Alcoholics. With the negative and hostile responses discussed, patients have little or no motivation to change their addictive patterns of behavior. These enabling behaviors by the therapist serve to continue the problem rather than solve it.

Transference can be seen as "the process whereby client attitudes formerly expressed or felt toward another person important to the client were unconsciously 'transferred' or projected to the counselor" (Brammer and Shostrum, 1982, p. 212). Therapists are not free of attitudes and feelings about their clients and, as shown in the previous discussions, are capable of projecting or "transferring" these onto their clients. This projection, since it is from therapist to client, normally falls under the label of "countertransference" and is likely to be seen as a reaction to the client's behaviors rather than as originating within the therapist.

The therapist reactions to alcoholics discussed are certainly extremes, but the counselor is likely to experience similar reactions to clients with problems other than chemical dependency. If these counselor reactions follow the same patterns, then it would seem to follow that the behaviors are codependent.

Family Systems Theory

Coming out of the physical sciences, General Systems Theory conceptualizes the universe as a unit rather than a group of component parts which act independently. The parts are important and need to be seen in their relationship to the whole as well as by themselves. The interactions of all the parts affect the actions and reactions of the individual just as the actions of the individual affect the whole system. General Systems

Theory seems to hold whether discussing chemical reactions, ecological relationships, or human interactions.

When this concept is transferred into the therapeutic domain, General Systems Theory can easily be applied to counseling. A person is not only an autonomous individual but is also a member of many overlapping systems such as family, workplace, city, state, and nation. If the client is examined outside of these systems, behaviors and attitudes may not make any sense; yet when examined within the content of the appropriate system, the patient's behaviors and attitudes become clearer. Therapeutically, the statement "the system is greater than the sum of its component parts" is true. Often the system which can be most readily and effectively utilized with clients is the family whether the family of origin and/or current family systems (Nichols and Everett, 1986).

Many of the concepts of family systems theory can be applied directly to codependency. As originally developed by Bowen, family systems theory contains eight concepts which are

- differentiation of self/fusion
- triangles
- nuclear family emotional system
- family projection process
- emotional cutoff
- multigenerational transmission process
- sibling positions
- the process in society (Singleton, 1982).

Of these eight concepts, the following ideas seem to be most compatible with codependency:

- differentiation of self/fusion
- triangles
- nuclear family emotional system
- emotional cutoff

Differentiation of Self and Fusion:

When working with an individual client or a client family, the therapist enters into and becomes part of a relationship. Within this relationship, all the dynamics of a system develop and are acted out. All members of the system, including the therapist, maintain an internal balance between fusion and differentiation. This can also be expressed as the balance between the immature, childish aspects (fusion) and the adult, mature aspects (differentiation) of an individual's personality (Singleton, 1982).

Another way to describe the difference between the two is by comparing the coping strategies of the individual.

> *Fusion is present when immediate comfort*
> *and gratification take precedence*
> *over the person's long-term goals.*

The individual is focused on reactions of others to self and is rigid and inflexible in interactions. Differentiation involves careful consideration and decision making, persistent pursuit of long-term goals with an acceptance of delayed gratification, and more adaptability and flexibility.

The solid self and the pseudoself are two specific terms which begin to tie in the concept of codependency. The solid self is the differentiated aspect of the person which has clear beliefs, attitudes, and values, changing only through a slow internal process.

> *The solid self recognizes differences between individuals and does not change just to maintain harmony and conformity in a relationship.*
>
> —Singleton, 1982.

The pseudoself, another name for fusion, experiences extreme discomfort when important differences of opinion are encountered. In the attempt to avoid such discomfort, such manipulative methods as an instantaneous shift of perspective to match that of the other person, concealing personal opinion, and debating correctness of opinion are used. The pseudoself reacts to emotional demands by pretense or acting to maintain harmony and peace. Under low levels of stress, individuals who are poorly differentiated can appear calm, responsible, and effective; however, under stress, the fused or pseudoself coping strategies appear (Singleton, 1982).

The behavior of the individual operating with a low level of differentiation compares directly with the behavior of a codependent. One of the diagnostic criteria listed by Cermak (1986a) is enmeshment in relationships with an individual with several dysfunctional behavior patterns, including chemical dependency. Cermak also listed boundary distortion in intimacy and separation as a characteristic of codependency. Enmeshment and boundary distortion are certainly typical of the undifferentiated individual.

Triangles

When two members of a system are in a state of fusion, a state of tension also exists. This tension can be increased or lessened through the involvement of a third party who takes sides for or against one member of the original dyad. The dyad automatically seeks to "triangle" this third party and the members of the triangle seem unaware of what happens in the interactions. Individuals who are well differentiated are better able to identify what is happening between the members of the group and able to avoid entanglement in triangles (Singleton, 1982).

If the tension is still more than the original triangle can cope with, an increasing number of triangles are formed until the stress in the original dyad is lowered to a manageable level. Singleton (1982) states:

This process can continue until personal triangles are exhausted and the tension spills over into the public arena of police, social workers and judges. A successful externalization has occurred when outside workers are arguing with each other, while the family is calmer. — p. 84.

Just as with the Drama Triangle from Transactional Analysis, triangles are examples of codependent behavior. Triangling is an example of the process a codependent might use in the attempt to gain control over a situation and the other member of the dyad.

Nuclear Family Emotional System

People tend to enter into marriages and similar relationships with individuals who function at the same level of differentiation as themselves. Of course, low levels of differentiation in the individual correspond with high levels of fusion. High levels of fusion in both partners present the potential for problems in the relationship. A highly fused relationship may alternately be described as highly enmeshed or entangled.

In highly fused relationships, dysfunction will sometimes appear in the "overadequate-underadequate re-

94

ciprocity" in which one member functions at a low level while the other partner assumes those responsibilities which the underfunctioning member has abandoned. The relationship will continue in this pattern until the underfunctioning member's complaints, ailments, and inadequacy begin to have a negative impact on the over-functioning member. In the extreme, the responsible member is likely to suffer physical, social, and/or psychiatric problems after a period of time. At this time the problem will be seen by both members as that of the underfunctioning partner (Singleton, 1982).

The "overadequate-underadequate" model of interactions corresponds well with the behavior of the "Enabler" who assumes the duties and responsibilities of the dependent as well as his or her own. At the same time, the "Enabler" is subject to stress-related problems as well as physical and emotional abuse.

Emotional Cutoff

Family systems theory advances the position that all individuals have some degree of unresolved issues with their own family of origin. The better differentiated the individual, the fewer unresolved emotional attachments there are which must be dealt with in later relationships. The person with many unresolved issues or poor differentiation establishes an emotional cutoff process which includes such things as denial and isolation or moving away from the family of origin (Singleton, 1982).

Clinical observations of families have shown that those families which are able to establish emotional closeness across generations seem to have fewer problems. At the higher levels of cutoff (fusion) more problems are noted, including diagnosable psychiatric disorders.

Individuals normally enter into long-term relationships with others who are at the same level of differentiation as themselves. Children tend to be differentiated at the same level as their parents, although the degree of triangulation between parents and each child creates varying levels of differentiation. This can result in the child being at a slightly higher or lower level of fusion than the family. The more intense the triangulation, the greater the level of fusion in the child (Singleton, 1982).

One of the adages about children of alcoholics is that they become alcoholics, marry alcoholics, or both. That maxim is supported by both anecdotal and clinical evidence (Wegscheider-Cruse, 1985). Cermak (1985a) notes that staying in a relationship with an active chemically dependent individual is one of the indicators of codependency. This tendency certainly seems to be the same pattern as that discussed in family systems theory.

Codependency and Systems Theory

These aspects of systems theory when compared with the diagnostic criteria advanced by Cermak (Figure 1) and with the descriptions of codependent behavior, beliefs, and attitudes advanced by Black, Wegscheider, and Baasel show numerous similarities. In fact, it seems quite possible that the same behaviors are described from different viewpoints—one with alcoholism/addiction as the prime focus and one without. The fusion described in systems theory matches the enmeshment and emotional entanglement of codependency.

To work effectively with clients, a counselor must be able to maintain a level of objectivity while being confronted with the emotional intensity of the therapeutic relationship. The better differentiated the therapist, the better that professional will be able to avoid emotional entanglement and the need to establish emotional cut-offs with clients (Singleton, 1982). This avoids codependent enmeshment with the patients.

One of the sometimes unrecognized aspects of the term "therapy" is the connotation of illness. People coming to a professional with their illness often present themselves as helpless. This is an invitation to the therapist to be helpful by taking over and running the client's life. This can also be a trap for the counselor as it fits the "over-adequate/underadequate" model in which the client needing help is seeking someone to assume responsibility for the problem and the solution. In terms of codependency, the helpless client is in the role of the dependent and the helper or overfunctioning member of the system is the codependent. This can develop into a circular system of escalating feedback and caretaking, with the therapist becoming more and more enmeshed with the client. Eventually this emotional entanglement makes the therapist subject to all the problems found in the undifferentiated or fused member of a family system.

Codependence from a Multi-Perspective View

Codependency can be viewed as one of several sub-syndromes of a larger underlying addictive process (Schaef, 1986). This underlying process is seen as being the fundamental base for all of the addictions, codependency, most psychiatric/mental health disorders, the dysfunctional family, and the chemically dependent family. Schaef sees each of these as separate diseases or problem areas which require specific but frequently similar treatments.

Characteristics of the Addictive Process

- Dishonesty (Denial, projection, delusion)
- Not dealing with feelings in a healthy way (frozen feelings; being out of touch with feelings; distorted feelings; holding onto feelings like resentment)
- Control
- Confusion
- Thinking disorders (ego-oriented; confused thinking; obsessive thinking; overreliance on linear, logical, analytic thinking; dualistic—either/or—thinking; perfectionism
- External referenting—being "other-directed" (low self-worth, "impression management," shame-based existence)
- Dependency issues
- Fear
- Rigidity
- Judgmentalism
- Depression
- Inferiority/grandiosity
- Self-centeredness
- Loss of personal morality (compromised value system, loss of a spiritual base)
- Stasis
- Negativism

Figure 9: From CO-DEPENDENCE: MISUNDERSTOOD—MISTREATED by Anne Wilson Schaef (New York: Harper & Row, 1986). Reprinted by permission of Harper & Row, Publishers, Inc.

She describes a large number of symptoms which she believes may be seen in those individuals who are affected by the addictive process. Any specific subsyndrome has many but probably not all of the symptoms. If the underlying addictive process is not addressed in treatment, the symptoms may return in another form. The characteristics of the addictive process are listed in Figure 9. The presence of the addictive process in the majority, perhaps even 100 percent, of individuals is a fundamental premise of her theory. Not all individuals are actively engaged in the process at any given time.

Many of these characteristics are also those of the codependent. It is relatively easy to see the adverse effects these behaviors and attitudes could have on a client or the therapeutic relationship. That relationship can probably never really develop if such characteristics as judgmentalism, rigidity, dependency issues, or thinking disorders are present in the therapist. The rest would have serious negative effects on the formation of an effective relationship.

Schaef theorizes that all of these problems have common characteristics although none are exactly the same. She states that the addictive process is an underlying disease which manifests itself in different ways, depending on the activating systems. She makes the point that there are multiple primary systems which impact on an individual, including the family, the individual within, the institutional system, and society at large (Schaef, 1986).

The effectiveness of recovering alcoholics
and addicts with the perspective of
"I've been there, so I know what it's like"
cannot be denied.

—Schaef, 1986.

Similarly, recovering codependents are able to work with other codependents with remarkable success. In both instances, the previous existence of a problem in the counselor appears to work to the advantage of the therapeutic process as sound recovery from the problem is modeled and discussed. The admission of the battle being fought and won by the therapist is seen as a strength. Therapists who do not have the problem also can work with these clients, but they often lack the personal knowledge of the real emotional impact of either addiction or codependency.

The success of the Alcoholics Anonymous and Al-Anon programs in helping individuals with problems of alcoholism and co-alcoholism has led to the development of Twelve Step programs for many of the problems people experience. There are Twelve Step programs for drug addicts, overeaters, spouse and child abusers, sex offenders, incest survivors, abuse survivors, people with emotional problems, and corresponding or joint programs for the "significant others" of the members. All of these programs are based on the premise that a person recovering from the problem is better able to relate to and help the individual who still suffers. In fact, "carrying the message to those who still suffer" is an integral part of the ongoing recovery program for those who honestly work to improve their own lives in these programs.

Many chemical dependency programs maintain a balance between recovering alcoholics/addicts and "non-recovering" therapists on their counseling staff. "Non-recovering" refers to those therapists who have never had a problem rather than to those who are actively practicing their disease (Schaef, 1986).

Contrast this with the conventional mental health program which focuses on the well treating the ill. Schaef states that the mental health system is based on the premise that a group of individuals who, by definition, have no "problem" diagnose and label others as having problems. The entire diagnostic system for psychiatric problems is based on non-involved, "healthy" individuals who are able to "objectively" look at the behaviors and attitudes of others and determine causal relationships. She sees this attitude as a form of denial on the part of mental health professionals about the addictive process, its proper treatment, and the therapist's own codependent involvement. These mental health professionals may not be trained in the problems of alcoholism and addiction or codependency and therefore are unable to detect and treat these problems in their case loads.

If, as discussed earlier, a minimum of 26 percent of the population is potentially codependent because of belonging to an alcoholic family, it is not unreasonable to assume that a minimum of 26 percent of any therapist's case load may be codependent. In actuality, when the symptoms of codependency as discussed by Cermak (Figure 1), Nelson (Figure 3), or Schaef (Figure 9) and the characteristics of Adult Children of Alcoholics proposed by Woititz are considered, the percentage may be much higher.

Chapter 4

Implications of Codependency

Codependency in the therapist is potentially a significant problem in the chemical dependency field at the very least, but also across the entire field of therapy. Based on the Pilat and Jones (1985) study using the Children of Alcoholics Screening Test and based on anecdotal data, codependency probably exists to a large degree in most other areas of the helping professions as well. This can create the same types of interpersonal and enabling problems in various mental health facilities and human service agencies as those which are seen in chemical dependency programs. Casner (1984) states:

Many of us choose human services to justify our need to help, do for, or control the lives or well-being of others. We professional helpers take great pains to channel our "helping" impulses into socially accepted and even admired routes. —p. 6

The untreated codependency of a therapist can and does lead to different and potentially greater problems than those most often seen with a recovering individual. The unidentified and therefore unrecovering codependent counselor has never learned new ways of coping with the issues of codependency as they surface and is not aware of the many problems which can result for the therapist, the agency, and the client.

For the Therapist

Many people come into the helping professions because of their unresolved codependency issues (Wegscheider, 1982, 1984) and when untreated individuals begin to work with clients, strange things seem to happen. They often find themselves rearranging their personal and professional schedules to fit a client's needs or desires (frequently on extremely short notice), feeling sympathy for families rather than intervening in negative cycles, and finally offering education and insight in place of action or confrontation because of a fear of meeting resistance from the family or the addict. The therapist who has unresolved codependency issues will become a part of the pathological system rather than an intervention in it.

A therapist's own codependency issues frequently will surface as the same behavioral symptoms displayed by an unrecovering client. Cermak (1986a) identifies these as "pride, shame, and doubt (p. 94)." The pride is in the power of therapy and the belief that the therapist has the power to control the client and the ability to manipulate the client into sobriety. Pride can result in the therapist taking credit for the client's progress. This can lead the therapist to a loss of self-worth whenever that client decides to return to old behaviors, including active addiction. Shame in the counselor is also a function of the client's behavior and return to compulsive and self-destructive behavior. When the therapist's self-esteem is tied to client progress, the therapist is modeling codependent behavior. Low self-worth in the therapist stems from the doubt of worth as a person, uncertainty about professional abilities, and the fear of the client's rejection. Therapists may also doubt their own professional skills and fear that others will judge them as incompetent as they judge themselves. The issues of codependency as discussed by Cermak have been adapted for the concept of codependent therapists and are shown in Figure 10.

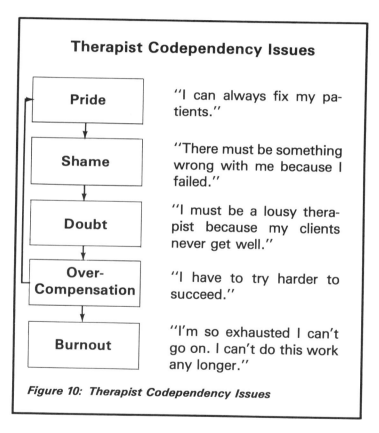

Figure 10: Therapist Codependency Issues

All therapists have these fears to some degree. The presence of these fears is not the problem; the counselor's denial of the fear creates the problems. The counselor who goes into the therapeutic relationship without recognizing or honestly dealing with these fears is the problem. While the therapist's conscious goal is to help the client, unconsciously the first priority becomes the relief of those fears. The counselor focuses on winning the client's approval and with treating the case "successfully," thereby not attending to the client's needs (Wegscheider, 1981).

Therapists who feel inadequate frequently hide behind a front of false professionalism, jargon, intellectualization, and impersonal interactions with clients in an attempt to prove to both patients and peers that they are truly effective. But when clients do not change,

---

There is an increase in the therapist's feelings of anger and guilt because of failure to motivate clients.

---

the therapist becomes increasingly frustrated as the result of even more proof of inadequacy. A therapist with low self-worth may find it difficult to nurture and give to a client what is not present in the counselor.

Neikirk (1984) talks of the therapist who gets onto a pedestal and is unable to get off. He describes some of the behavioral clues which indicate that a counselor is becoming "pedestalized." Some of the things he sees as indicating a problem include

- the helping professional who seems to have all of the answers
- a therapist who accepts without challenge a client's statement of how good the counselor is
- therapists who speak as if they know the "TRUTH"

106

- a name dropper in casual conversation or, even worse, during therapy sessions with a client
- a noticeable reluctance on the part of therapists to look at their own behavior or to work on noted personal and professional defects
- the counselor who won't talk about failures of therapy or who repeatedly talks during supervision of counseling techniques used rather than about the client or what the client does.

He also discusses four general characteristics which are seen repeatedly in those susceptible to the pedestal. People vulnerable to pedestal behavior

- have enormous needs for approval....
- struggle with lack of intimacy in their lives....
- have unrealistically high expectations of themselves....
- may subtly or unconsciously believe they are different and/or better than others.
  —Neikirk, 1984, p. 31.

He comments that these characteristics have been noted in children of alcoholics by Wegscheider, Cermak, and others. When these attributes are compared with the list of characteristics of Adult Children of Alcoholics listed by Woititz, the similarities are extremely obvious and Neikirk's concerns about these therapists become even more important.

Am I on a Pedestal?
Therapist Self-examination for Pedestal Behavior

1. When patients tell me how good I am as a therapist, I accept all of the compliments without challenge or clarification.

____Always ____Often ____Sometimes ____Almost Never

2. I give my patients feedback that leads them to believe I am right and which also minimizes any objections they might have to my behavior.

____Always ____Often ____Sometimes ____Almost Never

3. I mention names of well-known clients or authorities when talking with my peers or with clients.

____Always ____Often ____Sometimes ____Almost Never

4. I am unwilling to examine my own limitations, weaknesses, and personal or professional defects.

____Always ____Often ____Sometimes ____Almost Never

5. I don't like to talk about my failures as a therapist and when given the opportunity, I speak of my skills and techniques rather than how the client responds.

____Always ____Often ____Sometimes ____Almost Never

6. It is very important to me that people, both peers and clients, like me.

____Always ____Often ____Sometimes ____Almost Never

7. I have difficulty forming and maintaining long-term intimate relationships in my own life.

____Always ____Often ____Sometimes ____Almost Never

8. I understand and can accept that other people can and do make mistakes, but it is not acceptable for me to make an error.

____Always ____Often ____Sometimes ____Almost Never

9. I feel grateful that I do not have any of the problems that my peers and patients have.

____Always ____Often ____Sometimes ____Almost Never

Supervisor's Assessment for Pedestal Behavior

1. Does this person accept compliments from clients without challenging or clarifying the statement?

____Always ____Often ____Sometimes ____Almost Never

2. Does this therapist tend to speak in a manner which indicates that there is no possible alternative belief or position?

____Always ____Often ____Sometimes ____Almost Never

3. Does this counselor routinely mention the famous or important people he or she knows, has studied with, or has counseled, whether with peers or with clients?

____Always ____Often ____Sometimes ____Almost Never

4. Is this therapist open to feedback about personal or professional issues from peers or supervisors and does he or she take action on that feedback?

____Always ____Often ____Sometimes ____Almost Never

5. Does this counselor focus on specific techniques used in a therapy session rather than focusing on what the client says and does?

____Always ____Often ____Sometimes ____Almost Never

6. Does this person seem to have a great need for the approval of others, possibly going out of his or her way to gain that approval?

____Always ____Often ____Sometimes ____Almost Never

7. Does this counselor have difficulty bonding with patients and staff?

____Always ____Often ____Sometimes ____Almost Never

8. Is this therapist routinely unrealistically critical of her or his own professional performance by indicating an inability to complete a task because of lack of ability?

____Always ____Often ____Sometimes ____Almost Never

9. Does this counselor appear standoffish and intolerant of the behavior and attitudes of others?

____Always ____Often ____Sometimes ____Almost Never

Guggenbuhl-Craig (1971) points out that being totally engrossed in work and patients is a highly dangerous position for proper professional development as a therapist. Such immersion in the client and work often results in an inability to function in any kind of nonprofessional life. This situation may even reach the point that the therapist can talk of nothing but patients and work. Loss of the ability to love or hate, or to find excitement in life and the struggle to win or lose is the result. This individual finally comes to draw all emotional content from what the clients bring to the therapy sessions, thereby living vicariously on the patients' lives and relinquishing personal creativity and originality.

Guggenbuhl-Craig (1971) believes that a therapist needs to be completely interested in tracking both the personal and professional shadow. One of the things he believes to be important in this regard is the therapist's need to confront and deal with any fantasies held concerning clients rather than deny those fantasies.

He also believes that the more therapists examine their own unconscious, the blinder they become to new aspects of the self. After a while, they only reconfirm what they had learned previously. All therapists have a blind spot which blocks vision into new, dark areas of their own being. They also become unable to emotionally grasp what is known intellectually.

Still another aspect of the problem appears as the client projects negative, hostile, and aggressive messages onto others. The therapist responds to those attitudes and may begin to act out those responses (Davidson, 1977). Imhof, *et al.* (1983) point out that frequently this acting out may appear as
- chronic lateness for work or therapy sessions
- shortened sessions with clients
- getting drowsy or daydreaming during the session

•refusing to return client telephone calls in a reasonable time

These are just a few examples of how negative countertransference can be acted out by the therapist. If such behaviors continue to occur, they can be antitherapeutic and damaging to the counseling relationship.

Finally, some of the other aspects of the dependent/codependent relationship which may play themselves out in therapy sessions have been discussed by Wegscheider (1981), Hathaway (1983), and Cermak (1986a). A therapist can easily become overly entangled in the system with an alcoholic/dysfunctional family and will begin to assume responsibility for the alcoholic/addict or begin to sympathize with the enabler. The counselor may become "just like one of the family" and begin to fill a role in that family (Wegscheider, 1981, p. 223).

If the helping professionals came from a background in which they spent time trying to fix their family, they may re-experience the pain of that original family when working with another dysfunctional system.

These therapists may get so involved in trying to rescue the alcoholic that they forget to confront all of the client/system behavior which tends to support the continuation of the problem. They may also forget that the rest of the family is currently enduring the same type of pain as that which these counselors experienced in the past.

Furthermore, the therapist is always responsible for the development and implementation of a complete and ethical treatment plan.

Once this treatment plan is developed, if the therapist fails to follow through with it because of fear of client reaction, then codependent behavior is present.

The therapist again has become part of the problem and of the system of denial and enabling.

For the Agency

Over a period of time, agencies can develop a complex pattern of interpersonal behaviors which can be compared with the system dynamics of a family. Just as in a family, functional and dysfunctional dynamics are frequently found in an agency. When one or more members of the agency "family" are actively involved in a codependent process, the system dynamics take on many of the aspects of a chemically dependent family. In the offices of the mental health agency, the chemical dependency treatment unit or agency, and in the offices of many counseling services it is not at all uncommon to see interactions between the members of the staff which are similar to the roles taken by the members of alcoholic families (O'Connell, 1986).

Many of the dynamics seen in alcoholic families are found in the clinical staff of drug and alcohol treatment programs. This is not surprising since so many treatment professionals are adult children of alcoholics and/or recovering alcoholics and addicts; the behaviors are carried from the family of origin to the marriage family and also to the treatment or agency family

(O'Connell, 1986). Hathaway (1983) has noted that many treatment settings are an alcoholic family system in which the staff communicates inconsistencies, infighting, and passive-aggressive behaviors. Finally, White (1983) has noted that when the members of these organizational systems individually and collectively adapt to the internal problems, the organizational families of chemical dependency treatment programs follow the same patterns of isolation from the outside world.

As long as no crisis strikes the clinical staff which is functioning along the same lines as an alcoholic family, it will appear to function well. However, when a crisis or trauma occurs to that staff, the members will usually react with the "don't talk, don't trust, don't feel" model of behavior. This trauma can be the relapse of a recovering staff member, a severe illness, the promotion or transfer of a member, or a co-worker's quitting to move on. The head of the staff is usually the member who acts as the dependent or codependent parent and discourages talk about the trauma and expression of feelings while the other roles are assumed by various members of the family (O'Connell, 1986).

Susan

Sometimes this place really seems crazy. Tom is always on my case about my nurses. He runs hot and cold with his policy changes and his availability to assist me when I need it. He makes promises which are never kept. It is hard to trust what he says today because he is liable to change it tomorrow. He will tell me something about one of the other staff members and tell me not to talk about his mentioning it. I am pretty sure that he does the same thing with other members of the staff as well.

114

I really try hard to make this place work right. I pick up most of the slack in the schedule. I have been working extra hours every week to cover the holes in the nursing schedule. I work closely with the counselors so that the patients do not suffer from the craziness.

I don't know what to do about Sam. He gets harder to talk to every day. We used to talk together a lot, but he seems to spend more and more time isolating himself in his office instead of mingling with the rest of the staff. I think he might be drinking again, but even if he isn't, he seems very depressed.

Mary has been getting sicker and sicker in the past few months. Her time off has not seemed to help. I am afraid that she is getting burned out and is not willing to admit it. Her defensiveness is more noticeable now and her openness to feedback has disappeared.

Sometimes this place seems just like my home. People cooperate just about as well and there seem to be as many secrets. I get tired of carrying messages back and forth between people who seem unwilling to talk to each other.

Perhaps the ultimate codependent behavior a therapist may exhibit is enabling a peer whose performance is not up to professional, ethical, or legal standards. When a therapist has knowledge of unprofessional or unethical behavior on the part of another staff member or even a member of another agency and fails to confront the issue, codependent patterns of enabling are present. Among the behaviors which fall into this category are the following:

- a professional being sexually intimate with a client
- some other form of dual relationship with a client
- the professional's unresolved chemical dependency

- professional incompetence
- violations of professional association codes of ethics
- enabling behavior by the problem peer

These are just a few examples in which failure to confront a situation must be seen as condoning or enabling the behavior and therefore as codependent behavior. This example of codependent behavior impacts not only the impaired professional and the agency involved but that individual's entire case load as well as other clients in the agency. In cases where the unprofessional behavior is sufficiently severe, this type of codependency may adversely affect the entire profession.

White (1983) notes that it is not difficult to see that the staff of agencies which function along dysfunctional lines have high levels of stress-related and other health problems. Some of the symptoms which can be seen include:

- substance abuse
- loss of emotional control
- negative attitudes
- cynicism
- grandiosity
- hopelessness
- disruptions in relationships
- many physical illnesses

Continuing to work in an agency which is chronically understaffed or working in a situation with a constant undercurrent of tension are examples of codependent behavior between the therapist and the agency. A counselor who has to cope with the stress of both client and work system pathology is working toward "burnout" and may be the codependent therapist or a co-worker (Wegscheider, 1984).

Stillson (1986) has defined burnout as a "syndrome of

physical and mental exhaustion marked by the development of a negative self-concept, along with negative job attitudes and even a loss of concern and feeling for patients or clients" (p. 25). She notes that some of the common symptoms of burnout include such things as
- physical ailments
- loss of the sense of humor
- lack of motivation to go to work every day
- difficulty attending to clients in session
- anxiety/dread about working with clients
- an awareness of working hard and not feeling appreciated
- a growing belief that a patient cannot be helped and that it is not worth the effort to try
- an inability to fully relax when not at work

As the therapist gets burned out an additional problem arises—the problem of coping with feeling a perceived loss of competence when faced with such a difficult load. In addition to a lack of clarity about maintaining a sense of self-worth, it becomes increasingly difficult to know how to define the successes experienced.

Casner (1984) notes the high rate of burnout in the helping professions. She describes the characteristic symptoms of burnout as
- feelings of inadequacy
- feelings of frustration
- feelings of helplessness
- irritability
- depression

She asks, "When professional helpers develop burnout could this more accurately be termed codependent relapse?" (p. 7).

The development of codependent behavior on the part of one or more therapists certainly creates problems for the agency as well as the individuals concerned, but it also can be the cause of severe problems for the client.

For the Client

When the patient becomes aware of the existence of the counselor's shadow, the therapist is confronted with one of the ever present hazards of falling subject to the professional shadow. The invariable alliance between the client's destructive aspect and the therapist's charlatan shadow is difficult for the counselor to prevent. Unless the therapist is willing to confront personal shadow issues and also to risk admitting to the client that even the counselor is capable of backsliding into the unconscious, the client's therapy is endangered (Guggenbuhl-Craig, 1971). The image of the omnipotent, infallible therapist is impossible to maintain when the client has seen ample evidence to the contrary.

Through the process of identification,
the counselor may come to believe
that the only way the client can
recover is through the identical
therapeutic framework experienced
in the therapist's own recovery.

This limits the patient's options for recovery and also limits the therapist's effectiveness with the specific client. Imhof *et al.* (1983) discuss their concern with the possibility that the therapist may identify with the addict. The fact that there is an extremely large number of recovering alcoholics or addicts in the chemical dependency field is seen as significant. They feel that this process of identification is a specific countertransferential and attitudinal issue which may arise for these therapists and therefore for their patients.

Another concern expressed by Imhof et al. (1983) is a dissociative reaction that may serve to help therapists deny their own past, unresolved pathological behaviors. If this happens, the client may serve as an uncomfortable reminder to these therapists of that past. Rather than deal with residual issues of drug usage and related behavior, therapists may then terminate the patient's treatment.

In the game of "alcoholic," the therapist may be hooked into playing one of the game roles with the dependent member—Rescuer, Persecutor, or Victim (Steiner, 1971). The role of Rescuer is commonly adopted by therapists in the early dealings with a client when trying to provide guidance in dealing with work, family, and legal Persecutors. The Rescuer role prevents the client from having to successfully deal with the problems. In essence, the Rescuer tells the client, "It's okay, I'll take care of you and fix the problem."

When playing the Persecutor, the therapist, being conscious of the strong ethical taboos against persecution of a client, may become quite subtle in the means he or she uses in this role. One of the ways the therapist can be a Persecutor is by insisting that the client continue with therapy even after the client has given up the script for the presenting problem.

The therapist who gets caught in the role of the Victim is often the one who is consciously trying to avoid playing the role of Rescuer. The therapeutic victim is the counselor who permits theoretical discussions about the causes of drinking, transference and countertransference, unconditional positive regard, resistance, and dream interpretation. The alcoholic hooks the therapist into these extraneous issues and avoids the primary issue of alcoholism. This counselor remains unaware that the client is still drinking and apparently has no intention of quitting. This therapist, in the effort to avoid Rescuing, has been Victimized into enabling the client (Steiner, 1971).

The client who continues to drink is setting the therapist up to assume either a Victim role as described or the role of Rescuer. Another type of client who continues to drink between meetings is usually playing the "Drunk and Proud" variation of the alcoholic game and again is attempting to place the counselor in the role of Victim.

If the therapist is interested enough to challenge the out of office behavior then the client may stop the testing. Any therapist who believes that the client is still drinking and chooses to ignore that belief and instead deals with the client's underlying issues and problems is playing the game and is demonstrating codependent behavior.

Avoidance of the primary problem in favor of a secondary problem or symptom is always codependent behavior and therefore creates problems for the client.

The counselor who successfully avoids the trap and does not play the game and instead focuses on the drinking will make it possible for the client to stop playing the game and opt for recovery and treatment for the problem (Steiner, 1971).

A continual difficulty when working with addicted patients is the chronic, symptomatic denial of the severity of the problem. Dealing with denial requires a constant and direct firmness by the counselor who challenges this belief system. A therapist who is fearful of the reaction of a client is unable to help that client break through the denial and begin to work on the problem. Instead this counselor becomes too willing to see the patient's point of view and to accept all rationalizations, projections, and denials. This therapist does the client's bidding as a result of manipulation (Moore, 1961), and this becomes another enabling pattern of behavior.

The therapist who can be manipulated through fear of the client has fallen into the Enabling Trap! The counselor who joins the family in

- denial of the problem
- avoidance of the subject
- covering up for the dependent
- protecting from negative consequences of behavior
- and taking responsibility for the client

is practicing the same kinds of dysfunctional behavior as the family Enabler. This therapist has assumed the role of "Professional Enabler" (Wegscheider, 1981).

The Professional Enabler stands between the client and the crisis, the natural consequences of the patient's self-defeating behavior, which will motivate the needed changes in the addict's life (Wegscheider, 1981). The professional Enabler is most destructive when therapist codependent behavior teaches the client, individual, or family to reduce the crisis rather than to use that crisis as a stepping-stone into recovery (Kellerman, 1980).

Chapter 5

Resolution of Codependency Issues

Dealing with the Problem of Codependent Therapists

If codependency in therapists causes such problems, what can be done about all of these undesirable consequences? This chapter examines many of the methods by which a counselor's codependency issues can be identified and resolved. Suggestions for use by the individual, a supervisor, and a treating therapist are made and discussed. The flow chart on the following page indicates the various methods/interventions to be discussed and demonstrates the most appropriate point of application when working with the counselor with the codependency problem.

Identification

Having a means of quickly identifying codependent behavior in a therapist is a desirable objective. The problem encountered in diagnosing such behavior is the lack of valid and reliable testing instruments. Cermak (1986a) has advanced a set of DSM-III Axis II diagnostic

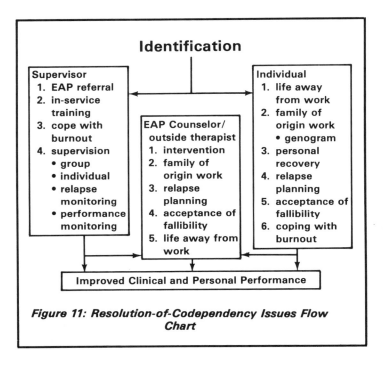

Identification

Supervisor		Individual
1. EAP referral		1. life away
2. in-service		from work
training		2. family of
3. cope with	EAP Counselor/	origin work
burnout	outside therapist	• genogram
4. supervision	1. intervention	3. personal
• group	2. family of	recovery
• individual	origin work	4. relapse
• relapse	3. relapse	planning
monitoring	planning	5. acceptance of
• performance	4. acceptance of	fallibility
monitoring	fallibility	6. coping with
	5. life away from	burnout
	work	

Improved Clinical and Personal Performance

*Figure 11: Resolution-of-Codependency Issues Flow
Chart*

criteria for codependency (Figure 1) with the recommendation that the criteria be put to rigid empirical testing. As yet, no studies have been published examining the criteria.

Pilat and Jones (1984) reported the use of the Children of Alcoholics Screening Test (CAST, Appendix 1) with a group of helping professionals which included therapists and counselor trainees. The results of this single study showed that children of alcoholics were 30 percent to 200 percent more common in this sample than in the original control group. This test can identify only those individuals who, because of a particular family background, have the potential for codependent behavior.

124

Friel (1985) published a preliminary Codependency Assessment Inventory (Appendix 2) as part of an attempt to develop a valid evaluation instrument. Results of studies using this inventory have not yet been published, but Friel (personal communication, October 1, 1987) states that the inventory has been informally given to several groups of therapists at seminars. When using the inventory with clients in chemical dependency treatment programs, average scores are in the area of 30-35 points. Friel states that counselors working on their own personal codependency issues score in the same average range. Since this is only a preliminary instrument, reliability and validity data are not available, but further investigation is warranted.

These tests seem to have the potential to help a counselor and/or supervisor identify codependency issues and the severity of these issues. While a preliminary diagnostic instrument is far from a final authority, for the purpose of preventing or working with codependency issues it seems well suited for the needs of the average therapist or supervisor in the development of a treatment plan. Once codependent behavior is suspected or identified, it then becomes necessary to take appropriate action to resolve the problem. There are several processes which can help in this corrective program.

Supervision

Probably the most commonly recommended method for recognition of, dealing with, and/or prevention of the appearance of negative behavior, including codependency, in therapists is good supervision. Clinical supervision is seen as a necessary and effective mechanism for the development and maintenance of clinical skills. Supervision is important if an agency is to deliver effective, efficient, and quality treatment services. It is valuable to help therapists deal with despair, frustration, and denial presented by clients and can also help reduce the high incidence of counselor "burnout" (Powell, 1980).

O'Connell (1986) suggests that "clinical staff should be encouraged to bring in an outside consultant on a regular basis and to increase these consultations if a 'clinical family' occurs" (p. 21). She also states that

departments of psychiatry are more likely to use outside consultants than are alcohol and drug programs — 75% of departments of psychiatry compared to less than 8% of alcohol and drug programs. — p. 21.

Stillson (1986), Davidson (1977), and Cermak (1986a) all agree with the concept of outside assistance/supervision to help cope with the problems of a therapist's codependent behavior. Guggenbuhl-Craig (1971) and Moore (1961) recommend that the therapist continue analysis and supervision by an experienced colleague as necessary to prevent or correct problems with shadowside or countertransference issues respectively.

Jack, Independent Consultant

Shortly after I began my assessment of the programs in the Chemical Dependency Treatment Unit, I became aware that the problems were not restricted to a single individual or individuals. The problems very obviously were interpersonal as well as personal and the intervention needed would be complex.

I could see that Tom and many of his staff needed attention. Some of the problems, primarily in the area of nursing, were legitimate personnel problems with inadequately trained or inexperienced staff and could be addressed through a series of in-service training sessions.

As for the rest of the staff, intervention was accom-

plished through a series of in-service trainings, thera-
peutic referrals, and confronting the dysfunctional
agency family which was present.

Peer group supervision is seen as a possible alternative to individual supervision. In this model, a structured group is developed in which various aspects of counseling are examined. Some sessions may be devoted to education processes while others may involve case presentation. The group format provides the counselor with emotional support, validation of work well done, feedback and suggestions for problem cases, and a sense of belonging and professional identity. The supervising therapist's time is more effectively used and the supervisee can be observed in a group setting. Stillson (1986) recommends problem-solving workshops of peers as a means of increasing the effectiveness of peer group supervision.

When the therapist is engaging in codependent activity, the supervisor is able to confront the negative behaviors and point out the effects of these actions on the counseling relationship and the client. Ideally, the supervision process will allow the therapist to examine the actions and consequences which result from the codependent behavior. The supervisor may help process insights and ideas immediately or may assign homework and other corrective measures for the supervisee to put into practice. The supervisor's primary focus must be performance related and interventions need to be at this level rather than at the level of the personal life of the codependent therapist. If the supervisor believes that the codependency is creating major problems or sees that immediate correction of the behavior is not happening, referral to an outside therapist for individual or group therapy for codependency is not only appropriate and desirable but may be ethically required as well.

Life Away from Work

Another important recommendation made by Guggenbuhl-Craig (1971), Small (1982), and Neikirk (1984) which can be very effective for the treatment of codependency as a therapist involves the therapist's private life. All three state that it is extremely important that the therapist have a personal life which is separate from clients and office. Guggenbuhl-Craig states:

In my opinion, and on the basis of my experience, there is one thing which can ameliorate or even dissolve the therapist's shadow-entanglement: friendship.... Friendship, loving but forceful encounters with one's equals, to attack and be attacked, to insult and be insulted—all of this strikes again and again at the psychic center of those involved. What the analyst needs is symmetrical relationships, relationships with partners who are up to his mark, friends who dare to attack him, to point out not only his virtues but his ridiculous sides. This kind of stimulation may be found with friends of the same sex; it can also take place within a marriage—the depths of the shadow must be plumbed in love.—p. 135.

At the same time Neikirk recommends that the therapist find the way off the pedestal by taking necessary risks away from work and peers. The process of accepting vulnerability and intimacy with other persons in a non-therapeutic relationship helps the therapist move toward improved humility and self-worth. The demonstration to oneself of the ability to relate to others on an intimate level, taking risks of self-disclosure and friendship, serves to increase self-esteem and confidence. The personal gain in confidence in situations away from work bleeds over into the attitudes and frame of reference at work and increases the therapist's ability to relate clearly, openly, and honestly with clients.

Family of Origin Work

Bowen (1978) indicates that the effectiveness of any therapist is affected by that counselor's level of differentiation in the family of origin. It is possible to actively seek a greater level of differentiation. Individuals desiring to develop a greater sense of self apart from the family of origin are encouraged to actively interact with that family. Among the steps recommended are establishing person-to-person relationships with each member of the family, developing increased objectivity about the family by becoming a better observer of the family and learning to control emotional reactiveness, and beginning to withdraw from the triangled emotional situations.

One way to accomplish these things is through multiple family visits in which the individual consciously works to establish new patterns of interaction with parents and siblings. Those times when emotions may be expected to be at high levels, such as holidays or even funerals, are the best for effectively relating to the family in new ways. At these times, the individual needs to maintain a conscious effort to remain objective and not react as much as other members of the family. This apparent detachment from the dynamics of the family allows the formation of new patterns of relationships between the individual and the other members of the family.

Establishment of a new relationship with the members of the family of origin is usually not easy. The presence of more than one member can inhibit the formation of a new relationship or can modify the relationship to include the others as members of a group—neither of which is the desired effect. The focus needs to be on the intimate personal relationship and the development of communications on a mature and respectful level between the two individuals; this may require a distinct effort to separate the family one member at a time (Bowen, 1978).

Genograms are a graphic method of displaying intergenerational family relationships and patterns. Some of the patterns seen on a completely developed genogram include repeated illnesses, alcoholism, weight problems, mental illness, and other dysfunctions. A thorough genogram can be developed by a therapist or by the individual seeking differentiation. Information can be added during counseling sessions or when remembered by the person. Attention should be paid to family myths and legends about relationships and important events in the family. A genogram can be compared with a time track which displays world, national, and local events of significance. This allows the relationships between family history and world events to be examined (McGoldrick & Gerson, 1985).

Personal Recovery

Therapists who grew up in alcoholic or dysfunctional families come into frequent if not daily contact with clients who exhibit the same denial, projection, and rationalization that the alcoholic parent or other dysfunctional family member displayed. This statement is based on the unknown number of individuals who come from families similar to those described earlier in which restrictive rules and corresponding survival roles are present. A significant percentage of clients who are seeing therapists will come from these homes. Based on the results of the Gallup Polls discussed earlier, at least 26 percent of these patients can be expected to come from homes where alcohol was a problem and there is no way to predict the percentage of individuals who might de-

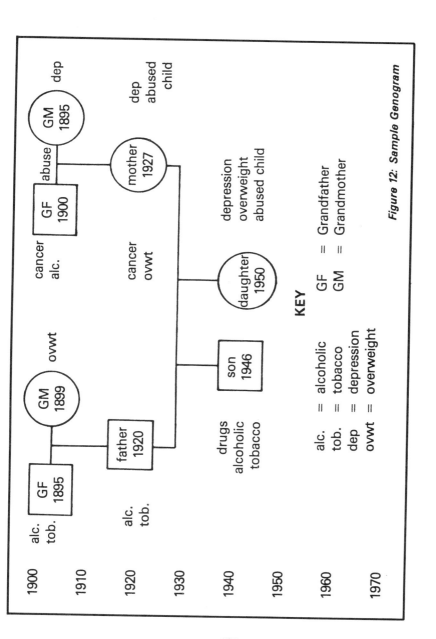

Figure 12: Sample Genogram

131

velop codependent behavior patterns as a result of other situations.

Susan

It was suggested that I attend all of the nursing in-service training sessions which included a lot of information on codependency. I was also to attend some Al-Anon and ACA meetings and report my reactions back to the consultant. He also referred me to a therapist who specializes in codependent families.

Boy, were my eyes ever opened. I learned that there are many people who came from the crazy kind of family I did. I have started regular attendance and am working on my issues. I also have begun working with the therapist he suggested I try. I don't have it all together yet, but I am beginning to feel that there is hope for me and this job.

As I have learned more about myself, I have been able to work better with my nursing staff. The consultant and I were able to develop a plan for in-service trainings and interventions for the nurses which has resulted in fewer problems between my staff and the patients.

One of the problems, which is also one form of denial common in the chemical dependency/codependency treatment field, is that posed by those professionals who are recovering from their own codependence. There is frequently a minimization of how much personal recovery is necessary before a counselor can begin treating others for codependency issues. Recovering alcoholics and addicts are routinely required by employing agencies to have a minimum length of sobriety before becoming chemical dependency counselors—up to two or more years. At the same time, many therapists who identify their own codependency issues are soon treating others for codependency (Cermak, 1986a), per-

132

haps thereby avoiding a resolution of their own issues. He also states:

If therapists hope to help clients understand codependency as the serious dysfunction it is, then those recovering from their own codependence must be willing to take steps to heal themselves first. Whether this occurs in a Twelve Step program, in therapy, or both—it will take substantial time and dedication—often as long as two years or more.—p. 94

Before treating others for codependency/Adult Children of Alcoholic (ACA) issues, the codependent therapist needs to have been working on a personal program of recovery from codependency for an extended period. Failure to do so may prevent the therapist from effectively helping the client to enter into recovery.

When seeking a therapist to help deal with issues of codependency, it is essential that the individual find someone who has experience with the issues of codependency and also has worked through his or her own personal problems in that area. This can be done by asking questions similar to those listed in the questionnaire which follows. If the prospective therapist is unable to give satisfactory answers to the questions, then it may be necessary to seek another counselor.

Questions to Ask Prospective Therapists
Anyone seeking a therapist for codependency issues should ask questions similar to these before committing to therapy.

1. How long have you worked with treatment of issues of codependency?

---

2. Do you identify yourself as codependent?

3. Are you involved in a recovery program for yourself?

4. What kind of program are you involved in?

5. How long have you been involved in that program?

6. How long have you worked with treatment of the issues of Adult Children of Alcoholics?

7. Are you the child of an alcoholic?

8. If the answer to No. 7 is yes, how long have you known about your own ACA issues?

9. Are you involved in a recovery program for yourself?

10. What type of program did you use to help resolve your own issues?

11. How long have you been involved in that program?

Coping with Burnout

Variables Affecting Burnout Rates

Casner (1984) not only advances the premise that

burnout is a codependent relapse but also comments that the methods of treating burnout are similar to the treatment plan for a codependent client. These treatments include learning to detach, establishing boundaries, increasing self-esteem, developing mutual support in the workplace, and being realistic about personal abilities and limitations.

Pines and Maslach (1978) have identified variables which can affect the development and outcomes of burnout on the therapist and the agency. These variables, both institutional and personal, are of importance when considering the negative effects of codependency on therapists. The personal variables include such things as the following:

Formal education—attitudes toward job and clients seemed to vary with the level of education of the therapist. Individuals with higher degrees seemed more negative about their work and saw little chance of helping many of their patients.

Rank—staff members who were higher in the organization of the agency seemed to have more negative attitudes about the patients and appeared to find fewer rewards in working with clients.

Time in mental health work—the longer the individual had worked in the mental health field, the more negative attitudes became and frequently the only good thing about the position was job conditions.

Sense of success and control—this variable seemed to correlate with the sense of having input into agency policies; this gave individuals increased self-confidence and good feelings about work and success.

Job attitudes—this related to working conditions, such as client load and administrative duties instead of patient contact, and the quality of interpersonal interactions between staff members. High degrees of satisfaction in this area seemed to indicate lower rates of burnout.

In addition to the personal variables which seem to be of importance, Pines and Maslach (1978) have also written about institutional variables which need to be considered when planning methods to deal with the problems of burnout in the agency. Some of these variables are:

Staff-patient ratio—therapists with many patients are more likely to dislike their job and are more prone to burnout.

Work relationships—affected by working conditions and by colleague attitudes toward work, patients, and the agency. Good relationships correlate to lower rates of burnout.

Frequency of staff meetings—the greater the number of mandatory meetings, the higher the discontent of staff, and the lower the quality of treatment provided.

Time-outs—the ability to withdraw temporarily to other work activities related directly to more favorable attitudes toward patients and lower rates of burnout.

Work schedule—longer work hours per day correlated with increased staff stress levels, decreased quality of patient care, and more burnout.

Time spent in administrative duties—the requirement to spend large amounts of time on paperwork resulted in increased dislike of jobs and the development of negative attitudes toward patients.

Work-sharing—work which was shared generally across the work force seemed to result in a perception of increased personal power in both private and professional lives.

Individual Responses to Burnout

Knauert and Davidson (1979) state that "Counselors

can, and must, counteract the stresses and prevent their own burnout" (p. 66). In dealing with issues of counselor codependency, the agency, the supervisor, and the individual therapist must all pay attention to the problem of burnout.

Casner (1984), Knauert (1979), Knauert and Davidson (1979), Pines and Maslach (1978), Beck (1987), and Valle (1979) suggest that the therapist find methods for meeting his or her own needs; failure to do so places the individual at risk of losing the caring and energy needed for treating clients. Among their suggestions is the need to find means to restore emotional resources; e.g., recreational activities away from work, professional conferences which give the opportunity to learn while giving the chance to relax, and fulfillment in private lives with activities which are not work related.

Next, they suggest that the counselor needs to develop methods of continuing to care for patients while learning to detach at the same time. Some of the methods discussed include intellectualizing client problems, learning to separate work and private lives by "leaving work in the office," finding methods to physically and/or psychologically withdraw from stressful interactions, and developing realistic expectations for oneself. Obtaining nurturing from reliable colleagues or other staff in a process of mutual support in the workplace can help prevent personal burnout as can the development of a staff group to work through interpersonal issues.

Finally, they see it as important that the counselor be able to develop a personal identity in the role of therapist. As discussed elsewhere, it is necessary to learn that the counselor is unable to "fix" or "cure" a patient. Practice in effective setting of limits with clients and learning to maintain personal boundaries with both patients and other staff is essential in this effort to establish that identity. Working with other staff to ensure that the case load for any individual is not excessive can be as important as learning to ask for help when needed.

Tom

I'm so glad that I called in a consultant. First of all, the training sessions have increased the levels of awareness of the problem for all of the employees. Many people have started looking at their own issues and interactions and are taking positive action. That alone would have been a successful outcome.

But the consultant also talked with me, pointing out that I and several of my staff were also exhibiting symptoms of burnout. He suggested that I seek medical assistance and therapy for my stress and other problems. We also developed a strategy which I hope will reduce the amount and probability of burnout in the agency. We will require all personnel, including me, to participate in stress management training, adjust work environment situations which contribute to burnout, and give staff members the opportunity to take time off.

Personally, I have been able to see that I have placed too much importance on the success or failure of this treatment program in my own evaluation of my worth as a human being. I have developed several hobbies which are very relaxing while not being work related. With my therapist I am working on learning to leave the office at work and pick up a whole separate life once I reach home. Finally, I have joined a group of other people who work as administrators in the various mental health agencies; we discuss the common problems we face and are working on solutions which will help with our problems.

Institutional Responses to Burnout

Knauert and Davidson (1979) also look at the role of the supervisor and the administration in preventing burnout in counseling staff. They note that the administration may occasionally find it necessary to require that personnel take advantage of educational opportunities as well as using accumulated vacation time since therapist overinvolvement with patients and work can result in burnout. They also indicate that the supervisor can establish staff groups which can be used to work through interpersonal issues among staff members. And finally they believe that the agency can establish a program of in-service training which can bring increased levels of professional knowledge and skill and therefore increased self-confidence and improved ptient care while reducing levels of burnout.

Pines and Maslach (1978) have identified several steps which any institution can take to help prevent the development of burnout in staff members. Some of the steps may take serious reorganization of personnel policies and management while others might be implemented rather easily.

- reducing the patient-to-staff ratio
- shortening the work hours
- allowing more opportunities for time-outs
- sharing the patient load
- changing the function of staff meetings
- improving work relationships
- training students to deal with future stresses

These things have the potential to make a significant difference in burnout rates in staff members and simultaneously increase the quality of patient care.

Codependency has a high risk of relapse for anyone working on recovery from the problem. Therapists who are codependent may relapse through the phenomenon of burnout. Both individuals and agencies can take specific actions which block this relapse into active codependent behaviors.

Relapse Prevention Planning

An important part of any program of personal recovery, regardless of the type of problem, is planning for the prevention of relapse into the problem. Smith and Gorski (1985a, 1985b) have advanced a developmental model of codependence, recovery, and relapse (Smith, Gorski, and Miller, 1983) which includes behaviors characteristic of all stages of the three aspects of the problem.

A recovery program needs to include reaching out for help, acceptance of the essential powerlessness of codependency, learning to cope with all feelings, detachment from the dependent member of the relationship, and development of a sense of self as an individual separate from others. Also as a part of recovery it is important to plan for the possibility of relapse.

This planning can be done by learning the warning signs of codependency relapse and developing an intervention plan for each of the four or five symptoms which are personally most significant. The thirty-seven symptoms of relapse into codependency which are presented by Smith, *et al.* (1983) are discussed here with a particular focus on codependent therapists.

1. *Situational loss of daily structure*—the therapist's daily routine is interrupted by temporary situations such as illness with a failure to return to all or part of normal work performance.

2. *Lack of personal care*—the counselor begins to place a total priority on caretaking clients and neglects personal recovery or needs to that point that she or he is second, third, or not at all.

3. *Inability to effectively set and maintain limits* — the therapist begins to be ineffective in setting limits with clients around therapeutic assignments and attendance at sessions.

4. *Loss of constructive planning* — the counselor begins to feel confused and overwhelmed by responsibilities with the result that the individual reacts to situations as they arise rather than planning priorities for projects.

5. *Indecision* — when confronted with the need to make a decision regarding client behavior, the counselor is unable to make that decision.

6. *Compulsive behavior* — the therapist begins to devote more and more hours of the day to client issues, treatment, appointments, and becomes a "workaholic."

7. *Fatigue or lack of rest* — the counselor has difficulty sleeping and frequently dreams about work, patients, or therapy sessions.

8. *Return of unreasonable resentments* — the counselor begins to attempt to manage feelings about a client and as the memories of the person's behavior are nurtured, the therapist becomes resentful and may even think such things as "Why do they always do this to me?"

9. *Return of the tendency to control people, situations, and things* — clients and co-workers are manipulated in the attempt to get them to do specific things.

10. *Defensiveness* — the therapist is quick to justify methods and course of treatment with clients even if unsure about the appropriateness and effectiveness of interventions used.

11. *Self-pity* — the codependent counselor begins to think such thoughts as "Why do my clients always do this to me?" or "Why can't I help anyone anymore?"

12. *Overspending/worrying about money* — the

therapist becomes concerned about fees, expenses, and yet may begin spending inappropriately and impulsively at the same time.

13. *Eating disorder*—the counselor may begin to change eating habits, switch to junk foods instead of the previous balanced meals, and begin working through meals instead of eating balanced meals at structured times.

14. *Scapegoating*—the therapist begins to blame colleagues or patients for the negative things and feelings which are happening.

15. *Return of fear and general anxiety*—thoughts of incompetence and inadequacy give rise to anxiety and nervousness in the therapist when entering the therapy setting.

16. *Loss of belief in a higher power*—the counselor may start to pull away from professional support groups, church, or God and begin to depend on self as source of strength.

17. *Attendance at Al-Anon becomes sporadic*—therapists stop regular attendance at meetings of professional societies, stop attending meetings of recovery support groups, and lose contact with necessary support groups.

18. *Mind racing*—even outside the therapy session the counselor spends large amounts of time and mental energy thinking about the problems of clients in the search for answers and insight.

19. *Inability to construct a logical chain of thought*—the counselor gets stuck on problems which would normally be simple which results in feelings of frustration and powerlessness; and the counselor becomes aware that her/his mind does not seem to work anymore.

20. *Confusion*—the therapist is unable to identify,

express, or even be totally aware of the feelings held toward particular patients and is unable to explain the resulting behaviors directed at that patient.

21. *Sleep disturbances*—waking up in the middle of the night following dreams about clients is common as is inability to sleep soundly because of thinking about patients.

22. *Artifact emotions*—unexpected anger and resentments directed toward patients appear for no apparent reason.

23. *Behavioral loss of control*—as the emotions arise, the therapist may begin to lose control of his/her temper and behavior with clients by yelling or punishing.

24. *Uncontrollable mood swings*—the counselor has changes in mood which happen without warning and seem quite dramatic or extreme.

25. *Failure to maintain interpersonal (informal) support systems*—the codependent counselor begins to stop reaching out to friends, family, and co-workers.

26. *Feelings of loneliness and isolation*—the therapist begins to withdraw from others and instead of dealing with the loneliness becomes increasingly compulsive and impulsive and believes that no one really cares.

27. *Tunnel vision*—the counselor focuses only on personal point of view and is unable to see the client's perspective.

28. *Return of periods of free-floating anxiety and/or panic attacks*—waves of anxiety seem to occur for no specific reason and may be so frequent and intense that the counselor is living in fear of being afraid.

29. *Health problems*—the therapist begins to experience physical problems such as headaches, migraines, stomach aches, chest pains, allergies, and rashes.

30. *Use of medication or alcohol as means to*

cope—seeking relief from physical and/or emotional pain, the therapist may begin to use illegal or prescription drugs or alcohol.

31. *Total abandonment of support meetings, therapy sessions*—the codependent counselor stops going to meetings and/or therapy sessions due to a variety of reasons such as a belief that the meetings are no longer needed, resentment, fear, or belief that they don't do any good anyway.

32. *Inability to change behavior in spite of conscious awareness that it is self-defeating*—the compulsion to continue in the same pattern of behavior in spite of knowledge that the behavior is not healthy begins to be stronger for the problem therapist.

33. *Development of an "I don't care" attitude*—the counselor begins to rationalize personal behavior as a lack of caring rather than admit that he/she is out of control. This results in the therapist beginning to ignore things which were once important.

34. *Complete loss of daily structure*—the belief that the counselor has an orderly life is lost, and the person finds that he/she is unable to perform simple daily acts of maintenance.

35. *Despair and suicidal ideation*—feelings that the situation is hopeless and that the only options left are going crazy, killing oneself, or getting drunk or loaded begin to appear in the therapist who is in the relapse process.

36. *Major physical collapse*—physical symptoms become so severe that the counselor can no longer function. These include ulcers, migraines, heart pains, heart palpitations.

37. *Major emotional collapse*—the therapist has tried everything to cope with and handle the unmanageability in life and becomes so depressed, hostile, or anxious

that he/she is totally out of control and unable to stop the behavior.

By involving significant others in the life and recovery program of the codependent, it is possible to preplan interventions to be used when any of the four or five most important warning signs are noted by those significant others. Such interventions may range from a simple verbal mention of the observation to a strong confrontation of the behaviors. The preplanning process also includes development of plans for confronting typical denial patterns. This intervention is intended to allow the relapsing individual to stop the behaviors before returning to the active problem state and then returning to active participation in a recovery program.

Acceptance of Own Fallibility

Possibly the hardest lesson for any counselor to learn is that the therapist is responsible for the development and use of counseling skills and the client is responsible for the decision to change. No matter how much the therapist wants to be able to make the client stop self-destructive behaviors, that change will not happen until the client is ready. This is not easy to accept. Many therapists working with addicted clients experience a strong and sincere desire to help in the belief that as therapists they know what the client needs to do to correct the problem. When this belief prevents proper therapeutic interventions, these same therapists are caught up in their own codependent behaviors.

One excellent way to learn how others change is through attendance at Al-Anon meetings. This allows the codependent counselor to hear how other codependents have learned to let the alcoholic be responsible. These support groups, combined with supervision and therapy for the counselor, will perhaps result in the realization that success comes in different forms. A success is not only the alcoholic who becomes abstinent and goes into a program of recovery; a success can also be the person who stays dry longer before relapse, the person whose relapse is of shorter duration than before, or even those clients who are better able to function in their own lives while continuing the problem behavior (Stillson, 1986).

Mary

This work with the consultant has been gratifying. I really thought that I was going crazy, but now I find that there is hope. The education from the inservice sessions was really great. I really saw the trap that I was falling into.

On top of my getting burned-out, I was also falling into the roles of Rescuer, Persecutor, and Victim. Lately I had been living most of the time in Victim and I hated it. Once I found out what was happening, I began to question what I was doing. I was told to begin to spend more of my individual supervision time focused on issues of my relationships with the patients and less on theoretical issues. When I did this, I began to see how many different places that I was being affected professionally by my behaviors.

I also began some short-term personal therapy with the goal of learning to accept the fact that I cannot be perfect and that not every client will do exactly what I intend. I hate feeling as if I can never do anything right, and I wish that I was perfect but I am learning that as I accept my own fallibility, I am also able to better accept the humanity of my clients.

Intervention and Treatment Plans

Johnson Institute Model of Intervention

Any action by a co-worker or supervisor which tends to break the dysfunctional patterns of behavior is actually a type of intervention. Simply noting that a behavior is happening may be sufficient to break the pattern, supervisory confrontation of an action is frequently effective, or a more formal intervention process may be needed. The process of intervention need not be the formal, planned action noted in the model discussed.

The model of intervention most often referred to in the chemical dependency field is based on the techniques developed by the Johnson Institute in Minnesota. This model has proved to be an effective method of intervention with many individuals who have a drug or alcohol problem and involves the following steps (Johnson, 1986):

1. Meeting with at least three of the people who are significant in the life of the addict.
2. Educate them to the various aspects of dependency.
3. Prepare them for an intervention, which includes written planning and history taking.
4. Practice the steps of the intervention.
5. Confront the addict with specific examples of behavior and the impact of those actions on the individual presenting the example.
6. Treatment for the dependency.
7. An ongoing emotional and social support system and aftercare program.

This model can be easily applied to a therapist or anyone else who is actively codependent. In this situation, the significant others are the co-workers and supervisor of the problem counselor. The terms codependency and codependent can be substituted for dependency and addict respectively. The intervention can focus strictly on work-related incidents with clients and other staff members and need not include the private life of the person, although non-work significant others and behaviors can be important in the intervention process and may make the process more effective. Treatment can include a formal program for codependency, private therapy, attendance at a support group for codependents, or any combination of these.

The close emotional bonding frequently found in "agency families" can present a barrier to the confrontation required.
—Jackson, Diaz, and Wallman (1979)

These agencies have become enmeshed, and the relationships between supervisors and subordinates resembles a peer group situation. It may be necessary to use an outside consultant to direct an intervention using this or similar models.

Employee Assistance Programs as Intervention

Another method of intervention which can be used with a codependent counselor is the Employee Assistance Program model. In this type of intervention, the problem behavior is addressed through the following steps:

1. *Observation*—the supervisor observes the counselor with the problem long enough to determine that there is in fact a problem.

2. *Documentation*—the supervisor maintains careful documentation of the work-related discrepancies and behaviors of the problem therapist.

3. *Counseling*—the supervisor meets with the codependent therapist, points out the specific work-related discrepancies which have been documented. The supervisor does not attempt to diagnose the problem; instead he or she focuses on the work discrepancies with specific counseling for desired change.

4. *Documentation*—once the original counseling session is carried out, the supervisor again observes and documents the problem therapist to determine if corrective action takes place.

5. *Referral*—if the codependent counselor does not change the problem behaviors, the supervisor meets again with the individual and points out that the problem has not been corrected. At this point the supervisor refers the therapist to the EAP counselor or another outside therapist for assessment and treatment.

6. *Follow-up*—supervisors are not expected to ensure that the impaired counselor is attending sessions or making progress in treatment or to assume any responsibility for the counselor beyond the normal range of supervisory behaviors. This supervision includes monitoring work-related performance with the appropriate documentation of continuing problems with clinical relationships and skills.

Referrals based on the Employee Assistance Program model are always an appropriate intervention with a therapist who is having problems with active codependency. Supervisor intervention with codependency is appropriate only at the beginning of the problem and only when focused on work-related or clinical issues.

Sam

I almost quit, I really did. When that consultant called me into Tom's office and talked to me, I almost walked out. I felt that he had no right to say the things he did. I've been sober for twelve years, and he implied that he thought I had relapsed.

However, after I got angry, I calmed down and was able to hear what he was saying. He reported some of the things I had said and done in the past few months. I could see why he and Tom might have thought that I had relapsed. I was on a heavy duty dry-drunk and was creating major problems with the nurses, the patients, and other staff, not to mention my personal life. The consultant then referred me to a therapist who specializes in the problems of late recovery, codependency, and helping professionals. My first reaction to therapy for codependency was that it must be irrelevant since I'm an alcoholic rather than a co-alcoholic.

Since I started going to that therapist, I have begun to learn that my addiction was only the first part of what I had to deal with in my life. Even if I had not been codependent earlier in my life, my responses to my work as a counselor have resulted in major codependency issues. Right now, I am seriously thinking about spending the next couple of years in a different job in the chemical dependency field which has fewer client contact hours.

The confrontation, using my job performance, was the only way that Tom and the consultant could have reached me. I had isolated myself so well that my therapist and I have had a terrible time finding ways past the defenses. I am beginning to think that the intervention actually stopped me from having that relapse.

Treatment Issues

Five general issues of treatment for codependency

have been identified by Wegscheider-Cruse (1985), and she has suggestions for treatment in each of these areas. These issues relate to all codependents, including therapists who are actively exhibiting these behaviors. She has identified these general areas as

- denial and self-delusion;
- compulsive behaviors including such things as workaholism, eating disorders, smoking, and other drug use;
- repressed feelings;
- low self-worth;
- medical complications such as most stress-related disorders.

The similarity between this list, the list of relapse symptoms, and the diagnostic criteria for codependency are readily apparent. These issues are important for the codependent counselor to resolve, as any of the issues can block delivery of effective and appropriate treatment to a patient. Denial of a problem blocks resolution of that problem, and self-delusion is seen in the belief that "I'm a therapist and I can handle this by myself. I'm not like my patients who need my help." Members of the helping professions frequently find it difficult to penetrate denial because of the feeling that they have more to lose—the role of the helper, the "omniscient" healer, or the expert (Korcok, 1982).

Compulsive behaviors such as those listed lead the counselor to avoid addressing the other issues of the codependency. The specific behaviors listed are frequently seen as a way to avoid having to deal with feelings. Addicts, alcoholics, and codependents have the common characteristic of not wanting to feel discomfort; when feelings which are disturbing come up, a common response is to try to find a way to change that feeling.

The easiest way to change feelings
is the way the person knows best—
the way practiced the most—
compulsive behavior or even addiction.

This can be a nearly automatic response to discomfort. In treatment and recovery the person needs to learn alternate methods of dealing with feelings.

When the therapist represses feelings about patients, whether anger, fear, happiness, or even sexual interest, rather than acknowledge the feelings, that counselor is building a reservoir of emotion which must be addressed in treatment of the problem. As a part of the treatment, this therapist must learn that having the feelings is not the problem; feelings of this nature are common. What must be learned is that it is not necessary to act on those emotions. Instead, the therapist needs to acknowledge the feelings in an appropriate fashion, sometimes with the client and at other times with a supervisor or in personal therapy.

Feelings of incompetence and inadequacy are very common self-esteem issues for codependent therapists which must be dealt with in treatment. The irrational beliefs of "I'm not good enough and they will find out" and "I'm a fake and they will find out one of these days" are fundamental self-esteem issues which can be brought out in treatment for codependency. The therapist providing treatment needs to plan methods for increasing self-esteem.

The physical complications which are apparent as a counselor becomes increasingly burned out need to be addressed both medically and through therapy. If the codependency is not addressed through counseling or some other means, the physical symptoms will return in the same or another fashion.

During the course of treatment for codependency all of these issues need to be addressed. Group therapy, along with appropriate individual therapy and education, is seen as an effective treatment method for most of these issues. The goal of treatment in all cases is recognizing the problem and beginning a program of recovery in each area. Establishment of an ongoing support system as part of a healing program is essential. A Twelve-Step Program such as Al-Anon or an ACA group is helpful for many individuals; other support groups also work if they are fully used by the codependent.

Adult Children of Alcoholics Core Issues

Gravitz and Bowden (1985) have advanced a list of core issues which must be addressed in the treatment of Adult Children of Alcoholics and other survivors of dysfunctional families. Some of these issues were identified by Brown and Cermak (1980) in their research with Adult Children of Alcoholics and the rest were identified by Gravitz and Bowden. These issues which must be addressed in treatment are

- issues of control/fear of being out of control
- issues of trust/distrust
- avoidance of feelings/belief that feelings are wrong or bad
- being overly responsible
- tendency to ignore personal needs in favor of others
- all-or-none functioning
- dissociation
- "adrenalin junkies"
- low self-esteem

Again it can be seen that this list is similar to the previous discussions of codependent behaviors and the attitudes of adult children of alcoholics. The importance of these core issues if the therapist in the counseling relationship is actively codependent in that relationship needs to be discussed. The problem of low self-esteem in the counselor has already been presented in this chapter. Note that many of the characteristics listed are ways individuals try to increase their own self-esteem at the expense of others or even themselves.

A counselor who has issues of control may manipulate the therapy session in such a manner that clients never

- get the opportunity to work on the issues the therapist is not comfortable with
- are allowed to work through the emotions the therapist fears most
- experience the full potential of a new relationship and thereby never gain one of the positive results of therapy relationships

This therapist needs to be able to resolve issues of control in order to be able to help clients work through their own issues, and that is best done through a formal program of therapy or a Twelve Step program.

An unwillingness to trust others is frequently an indicator of a distrust of self as well. A therapist who is unable to trust his or her own judgment will have difficulty projecting confidence in the client's ability to change. Further, this lack of trust in self may result in reluctance to attempt some interventions with clients. Again problems with trust need to be addressed in a formal treatment plan.

Therapists who try to avoid feelings in the therapy session are soon not genuine in their interactions with patients. By working to gain acceptance of feelings through therapy or some other program, the counselor regains the ability to be natural and spontaneous with friends, family, and clients.

The therapist whose codependence takes the form of being overly responsible prevents clients from learning to take responsibility for themselves. This is a subcategory of control, as the counselor feels more in control of the entire situation when assuming responsibility for the client. The process of learning to "let go" of the responsibility for the result is a difficult one and frequently follows a pattern of confrontation of the behavior and attempts to change, followed by more confrontation. Some of this confrontation can be done by a supervisor on a daily basis, but the major work needs to be done outside of the work situation through personal therapy.

Codependence and martyrdom seem to be concepts which are made for each other. A therapist whose behavior says, "The client's needs always come ahead of my own feelings and needs," is the person who never takes time off even if sick and never takes a vacation because "The patients might need me when I'm away." Through therapy, this counselor needs to learn to strike a balance between personal needs and the needs of a client.

In "all-or-none" functioning, the therapist is unable to see any middle ground and frequently operates with a set of expectations for self and others which are unrealistic in nature. This counselor either sees clients as successes or failures, interventions attempted as either successes or failures, and herself/himself as either a success or a failure. This person needs to learn to redefine success to incorporate some smaller, midpoint target goals and to allow others the ability to determine their own level of functioning. Again this can be done through personal therapy and/or a personal recovery program.

The therapist who separates the emotions aroused in

the therapy setting from the events of that session is dissociating. Again this can result in a counselor who is not genuine in the counseling session, one whose behavior or effect is not appropriate to the content and context of the session. Through therapy, this therapist needs to learn to reconnect the feelings to the event so that a consistent message is sent in interactions with the client.

"Adrenalin junkies" thrive on crisis and if there is no crisis, they create one. If a therapist is functioning in this fashion, interactions with colleagues and possibly patients are likely to be very inconsistent. Through a program of recovery which may include therapy, this counselor needs to begin to learn that calm and serenity are both desirable and achievable goals for personal mental and spiritual health.

These core issues certainly need to be addressed in the development of a treatment plan, and appropriate recommendations should be made to help to resolve the situations created by these issues. Supervisors can help with some of the treatment as can co-workers, but many of the issues need to be addressed through a formal program of recovery. This can include such things as personal therapy, either individual or group, and membership and participation in a Twelve Step recovery program such as Al-Anon or an Adult Children of Alcoholics group.

Treatment Plan

The following sample treatment plan is designed for a supervisor's information and for the counselor providing treatment to use with a codependent therapist, but it can easily be generalized for any client with similar issues. The plan does not include a planned intervention but could easily be modified to incorporate an intervention. The format discussed is considered effective to bring the codependent counselor to the point that he or she will be willing to consider the problem and possible solutions. Once the individual has started to accept the possibility of codependency issues, the treatment plan can be implemented. No specific exercise or technique is preferred over another; the therapist working with the codependent individual should use those methods which experience has shown to be most effective.

The parts of the treatment plan are not discrete, sequential procedures, but may overlap on each other. One exercise may impact on more than one area of the plan and with the exception of Step A (diagnosis) may be used in any order. This procedure can be effective when applied as part of routine supervision if the problem is seen as relatively minor or as part of a therapy program. Some of the parts of the plan can be easily used as part of a group supervision program with interns and other staff as well as part of an individual program of recovery.

Treatment Plan for Codependent Therapists

A. Such preliminary diagnostic aids as the Children of Alcoholics Screening Test and the Friel Codependency Assessment Inventory should be used to clarify specific issues relating to codependency.

B. Self-esteem exercises and assignments with specific attention to feelings of incompetence and lack of confidence as a therapist.

C. Assertiveness training and practice to include peer interaction and client-therapist situations as well as non-work situations.

D. Education about dependency, codependency, recovery, and relapse.

E. Stress management/relaxation training with special emphasis on imaging stressful client situations.

F. Development of an emotional and social support system such as Al-Anon or other recovery programs.

G. Development or improvement of non-work-related social and recreational activities.

H. Supportive confrontation of codependent behavioral patterns. This type of confrontation is caring and ongoing, pointing out potential relapses, self-defeating behaviors, and reenforcing positive change. Confrontation, in this sense, does not have to be a Synanon or Gestalt hot seat situation to be effective.

I. Develop a multigenerational genogram with special attention paid to patterns of self-defeating behaviors, stress-related illness, or other dysfunctions.

J. Be aware of personal and family secrets such as drug or alcohol abuse, insanity, child or spousal abuse, sexual abuse including incest. Enter these secrets in the genogram. Develop specific plans for these issues.

K. Deal with the feelings of pain, anger, rejection, loneliness, powerlessness, helplessness, and hopelessness. This will release the ability to experience joy, happiness, calm, serenity, self-confidence, friendship, hopefulness, and competence.

L. Develop a relapse prevention plan. Identify and plan for personalized warning signs in the work/client therapist setting.

Figure 13: Treatment Plan for Codependent Therapists

In-service Training Program

In-service training programs can also serve as a means of prevention and intervention in a problem. Issue-oriented workshops can be presented at routine staff meetings, using a member of the staff to present the information and facilitate the discussion. Alternately, an outside consultant may be used to provide the needed expertise to make the desired presentation. An outside consultant is the most effective intervention in the situation where a "clinical family" is developing dysfunctions and codependent behavior is an aspect of the dysfunction.

The following outline for an in-service training program has been used by the author in a combined interactive/didactic format. It is roughly based on the information in this book and can be presented in one or more sessions. The subject can be covered briefly in about ninety minutes. A three-hour or longer presentation or series of shorter presentations can cover the material in greater depth. Preparation for the training session should include thorough review of materials, development of handout materials appropriate to the audience needs, and provision of a reading list also geared to the requirements of the agency.

The Codependent Therapist

In-service Training Plan

I. The therapeutic relationship
   A. importance of client/therapist relationship
   B. similarity to all other relationships
   C. possibility of dysfunction

II. Review of codependency
   A. system with rules
   B. pattern of traits
   C. diagnostic criteria
   D. enabling behaviors
      1. avoiding and shielding
      2. attempting to control
      3. taking over responsibilities
      4. rationalizing and accepting
      6. rescuing and subserving
   E. self-esteem
   F. choose career in the helping professions
      1. ACA research
      2. CAST

III. Codependent therapist behavior
   A. enabler/rescuer
   B. supports addictive behavior
   C. burnout/relapse
   D. protect from negative consequences

IV. Theoretical viewpoints
   A. Transactional Analysis
      1. Rescuer

        2. Persecutor
        3. Victim
        4. Drama Triangle
    B. Jungian/Shadow
        1. Charlatan/Quack
        2. False Prophet
        3. Archetypes
    C. Psychodynamic—Transference/counter-transference
    D. Family Systems Theory
        1. Differentiation/Fusion
        2. Triangles
        3. Nuclear family emotional systems
        4. Emotional cutoff
    E. Addictive processes

V. Codependent therapist as a problem
    A. For therapist
        1. recovering/unrecovering
        2. shame, doubt, low self-esteem
        3. "pedestal" behavior
        4. burnout
        5. relapse
        6. over-invested in clients
        7. joins family system
    B. For the agency/treatment family
        1. development of dysfunctional dynamics
        2. crisis reactions
        3. high rate of stress-related illness
        4. burnout
        5. professional coverup

    C. For the client
        1. therapist identification
           a. punitive, terminate
           b. only one way to recover
        2. therapist hooked into system
           a. fail to confront behavior
           b. persecutor, rescuer, victim
        3. therapist afraid of client
           a. denial unchallenged
           b. manipulations work
           c. protects client
           d. keeps client from experiencing consequences

VI. Solutions to the problem
    A. Identification
        1. Cermak's criteria
        2. CAST
        3. Friel Codependency Assessment Inventory
    B. Supervision
        1. individual/group
        2. outside consultant
        3. in-service training
    C. Attention to therapist personal needs
        1. life away from agency
        2. non-professional/non-work relationships
    D. Family of origin work
        1. Family visits
        2. Genograms
    E. Program of recovery
        1. Al-Anon

        2. ACA group
        3. other support system

    F. Coping with burnout
        1. Variables
        2. Individual Responses
        3. Institutional responses
    G. Relapse Prevention Planning
        1. 37 warning symptoms
        2. Intervention plan
    H. Redefine success
        1. therapist not responsible for outcome
        2. longer periods between relapses
        3. shorter, less severe relapses
        4. improvement in level of functioning in
           life
    I. Intervention and Treatment Plans
        1. Johnson Institute Model of Intervention
        2. Employee Assistance Programs
        3. Treatment Issues
        4. ACA core issues
        5. Treatment Plan

Figure 14: The Codependent Therapist: In-service Training Plan

Visual aids such as charts, outlines, or illustrations can be prepared based on the outline. A sample visual aid is presented in Figure 15. A series of charts or transparencies based on the outline can be effectively used to help present this information to the clinical staff or service providers at any mental health, social service, or chemical dependency agency.

A good in-service training program can serve the dual

purpose of primary intervention with a codependent therapist at the same time that co-workers are taught to identify and treat the dysfunction. However, it cannot be assumed that the in-service training will provide all of the assistance the impaired counselor and staff need. The training provides the required education; the supervisor needs to implement the remainder of the treatment plan as appropriate.

Codependent Therapist Behavior

- **Enabler**
    - Rescuer
    - Persecutor
    - Victim

- **Supports Addictive Behavior**
    - Makes it easy to continue
    - Alcoholic's accomplice

- **All-Powerful—Can Cure Anyone**

- **Burnout**
    - Relapse

- **Protects Client from Negative Consequences**

Figure 15: Sample Visual Aid for In-Service Presentation

Chapter 6

Summary, Limitations, and Recommendations

Active codependent behavior in the therapist has the potential for creating problems for that counselor, the agency at which the therapist works, and for the client.

Effect of Codependent Therapists

Therapists are responsible for the skills they possess, the proper application of these skills, the types of interventions and referrals made, and for ethical behavior. If the counselor has kept these things in mind, responsibility for the results of therapy lies with the client as it is the client who determines success or failure by choosing to follow or ignore interventions. Regardless of theoretical orientation, therapists are susceptible to codependent attitudes and behaviors. The "Professional Enabler" is a title which can be given to those therapists who come to believe in the ability to transform a client into something or someone different. The same can be said of the counselor who assumes responsibility if the patient returns to negative behavior patterns.

The therapist who engages in enabling behaviors becomes a part of the dysfunctional system and reinforces denial—in fact becomes an accomplice or ally of the client. This results in the counselor's unintended collusion with all the other enablers in the system to protect the patient from experiencing negative consequences of behavior. This enabling can create several problems for the client and can be destructive to the establishment and maintenance of a sound therapeutic relationship.

Therapists who fall into codependent behavior may eventually experience periods of burnout, depression, or substance abuse problems. These are just a sample of the problems that codependent counselors experience as a result of their codependency. Other problems include feelings of inadequacy as a therapist, failure with clients, and fear of discovery as incompetent.

Agencies employing these counselors can develop the characteristics of a dysfunctional family with all of the negative dynamics which that implies. Increasing levels of stress-related illness are common in these agencies as are increased irritability and poor communications. Other members of the treatment team may experience some of the same symptoms as the problem co-worker.

Patients of a therapist who is actively codependent also experience problems as a result. Among these are poor therapy, inadequate resolution of the presenting problem, and enmeshment in another dysfunctional system with the therapist.

Solutions to the Problem

The problems caused by the presence of codependent behavior in the therapist are not necessarily insoluable. Identification of the problem behavior is possible and, once identified, there are several possible actions that can be initiated by supervisors and counselors.

The supervision process offers an excellent tool for monitoring and intervening in the problem. Both individual and group supervision are effective. Personal therapy and/or involvement in a support system are excellent parts of a program of recovery from codependence. The individual may need to resolve residual issues from the family of origin through visits or therapy.

Establishment of a life away from work and clients is essential to prevent burnout and the development of further codependent traits. Acceptance of personal fallibility and planning for relapse prevention are also important parts of the solution to the problem.

A more formal intervention and treatment program may need to be implemented by the supervisor to stop the behavior and to ensure that the counselor is taking appropriate action to resolve the problem. There are several issues of codependency which need to be addressed as a part of this treatment process, including self-esteem, confidence, and self-defeating behaviors.

An excellent part of the treatment plan for an agency which has developed the dynamics of a dysfunctional family is some form of training about the problem of codependency and the therapy session. An agency with this problem is strongly advised to seek the services of an outside consultant who does not have emotional investment in the current system for the purpose of determining the appropriate interventions for the staff.

Limitations of the Study

There are several limitations which affect this study. First, not all theories of personality and therapy were examined to determine concepts and constructs which correspond to those of codependency. It is possible that some theories might contain concepts which tend to refute those advanced here.

The second major limitation of this study is the lack of empirical data to support the hypothesis that codependent behavior by the therapist can cause problems for the counselor, the client, and the agency. Studies are needed to determine the validity of the diagnostic criteria and the incompletely tested diagnostic instruments. These studies need to be done with both the specific population of therapists and also with the general population.

The third limitation is that much of the data available on the subject of codependency is based on anecdotal and clinical experience. The large number of books currently on the market about codependency are based on therapist observation and client self-reports of the problems experienced. As noted in the discussion on the lack of empirical data, the lack of research data presents a significant limitation on the present study.

Recommendations

Further use of the Friel Codependency Assessment Inventory (CAI) and the Children of Alcoholics Screening Test (CAST) is needed within the clinical community. Both of these instruments have the potential to aid in the identification of codependent therapists and in the development of a treatment plan for these counselors. However, until the number of actual vs. potential codependent therapists is determined the extent of the problem will remain unrecognized.

Research to determine the validity of Cermak's criteria for codependency is needed. If his hypothesis is proved accurate, the addition of a recognized DSM-III-R diagnosis for codependency will do much to legitimize the concept and may result in improved research into all aspects of the problem. Furthermore, intervention with therapists who are codependent may be much easier if the criteria are validated.

Since the literature supports an extended period of sobriety or recovery from codependence before working with those specific issues, it is recommended that additional studies be designed to empirically test the validity of that requirement. Anecdotal data about the use of recovering alcoholics is readily available as are some published studies. The value of a recovering chemically dependent person as a therapist has been demonstrated numerous times, but additional studies need to be made to support the need for personal recovery from codependency.

References

Baasel, P. (1986). Passing down the heritage of addictive family dynamics. *Focus on Family and Chemical Dependency:* vol. 9 no. 6: 24, 25, 36, 39.

Beck, D. (1987). Counselor burnout in family service agencies. *Social Casework:* vol. 68 no. 1: 3-15.

Black, C. (1981). *It Will Never Happen to Me,* Denver, Col. M. A. C.

Bowen, M. (1978). *Family Therapy in Clinical Practice.* New York: Jason Aronson.

Brammer, L. & Shostrom, E. (1982). *Therapeutic Psychology,* 4th ed., Englewood Cliffs, N.J.: Prentice-Hall.

Brown, S. & Cermak, T. (1980). Group Therapy with the adult children of alcoholics. *Newsletter from the California Society for the Treatment of Alcoholism and Other Drug Dependencies:* vol. 7 no. 1: 1-6.

Casner, C. (1984). The co-dependent style: a gender and professional liability? paper presented at the *Ninth Annual California Conference on Alcohol Problems.* Carmel, Cal: Brightside ACT Center.

Cermak, T. (1986a). *Diagnosing and Treating Co-Dependence,* Minneapolis, Minn.: Johnson Institute Books.

Cermak, T. (1986b). Diagnostic criteria for co-dependency. *Digest of Addiction Theory and Application:* vol. 5 no. 3: 5-15.

Davidson, V. (1977). Transference phenomena in the treatment of addictive illness: love and hate in methadone maintenance. In J. Blaine & D. Julius (Eds) *Psychodynamics of Drug Dependence NIDA Research Monograph 12* (Rockville, Maryland: National Institute on Drug Abuse).

DiCicco, L. (1979). Children of alcoholic parents: issues in identification. In National Institute on Alcohol Abuse and Alcoholism, *Services for Children of Alcoholics, Research Monograph: No. 4.* Rockville, Maryland: NIAAA.

Dixon, T. (1986). Enabling: good intentions and the 'no-win' game of addiction. *Focus on Family and Chemical Dependency:* vol. 9 no. 1: 33-35.

Friedman, R. (1985). Making family therapy easier for the therapist: burnout prevention. *Family Process:* vol. 24 no. 4: 549-554.

Friel, J. (1985). Co-dependency Assessment Inventory. *Focus on Chemically Dependent Families:* vol. 8 no. 3: 20-21.

171

Gallup, G. (1986). An American paradox. *Alcoholism & Addiction:* vol. 6 no. 6: 18.

Gierymski, T. & Williams, T. (1986). Codependency. *Journal of Psychoactive Drugs:* vol. 18 no. 1: 7-13.

Gravitz, H. & Bowden, J. (1985). *Recovery: A Guide for Adult Children of Alcoholics.* New York: Simon & Schuster, Inc.

Guggenbuhl-Craig, A. (1971). *Power in the Helping Professions* New York: Spring Publications.

Hathaway, J. & Dennison, A. (1983). Family treatment: changing concepts in healing. *Focus on Alcohol and Drug Issues:* vol. 6 no. 4: 6-7, 30.

Imhof, J., Hirsch, R. & Terenzi, R. (1983). Countertransferential and attitudinal considerations in the treatment of drug abuse and addiction. *The International Journal of the Addictions:* vol. 18 no. 4: 491-510.

Jackson, G., Diaz, L. & Wallman G. (1979). An employee alcoholism program for nurses and social workers. *Labor-Management Alcoholism Journal:* vol. 9 no. 3: 115-122.

Johnson, V. (1986). *Intervention.* Minneapolis, Minn.: Johnson Institute Books.

Johnson Institute (undated). *The Enabler: The Companion to Chemical Dependency.* (available from [Johnson Institute, Minneapolis, Minn.]).

Jones, J. (1985). *Children of Alcoholics Screening Test: Test Manual.* Chicago, Ill. Camelot Unlimited.

Kellerman, J. (1980). *Alcoholism: A Merry-Go-Round named Denial.* (available from Hazelden Foundation, Center City, Minn.).

Knauert, A. (1979). The treatment of alcoholism in a community setting. *Family and Community Health:* vol. 2 no. 1: 91-102.

Knauert, A. & Davidson, S. (1979). Maintaining the sanity of alcoholism counselors. *Family and Community Health:* vol. 2 no. 2: 65-70.

Korcok, M. (1982). The healers are human too. *Focus on Alcohol and Drug Issues:* vol. 5 no. 3: 2.

Levinson, V. & Straussner, S. (1978). Social workers as "enablers" in the treatment of alcoholics. *Social Casework: The Journal of Contemporary Social Work:* vol. 59: 14-21.

McGoldrick, M. & Gerson, R. (1985). *Genograms in Family Assessment.* New York: W. W. Norton & Company.

Moore, R. (1961). Reaction formation as a countertransference phenomenon in the treatment of alcoholism. *Quarterly Journal of Studies on Alcoholism:* vol. 22: 481-486.

National Institute on Alcohol Abuse and Alcoholism. [NIAAA]. (1980). *Alcohol and the Family.* Rockville, Maryland: Author.

Neikirk, J. (1984). Getting off the professional pedestal. . . dare to be average. *Focus on Family and Chemical Dependency:* vol. 7 no. 3: 26, 28, 31.

Nelson, C. (1985). The styles of enabling behavior. In D. Smith & D. Wesson (Eds), *Treating the Cocaine Abuser* (pp. 49-71). Center City, Minn. Hazelden Foundation.

NIAAA. (1983). *Fifth Special Report to the U. S. Congress on Alcohol and Health.* Rockville, Maryland: Author.

Nichols, W. & Everett, C. (1986). *Systemic Family Therapy* New York: Guilford Press.

O'Connell, K. (1986). Counseling the counseling family. *Alcoholism and Addiction Magazine:* vol. 6 no. 5: 21-22.

Pilat, J. & Jones, J. (1985). Identification of children of alcoholics— two empirical studies. *Alcohol Health and Research World:* vol. 9 no. 2: 27-33, 36.

Pines, A. & Maslach, C. (1978). Characteristics of staff burnout in mental health settings. *Hospital and Community Psychiatry:* vol. 29 no. 4: 233-237.

Policinski, H. (1986). Family caretakers. . . professional caretakers. *Focus on Family and Chemical Dependency:* vol. 9 no. 6: 20-21.

Powell, D. (1980). *Clinical Supervision: Skills for Substance Abuse Counselors—Manual.* New York: Human Sciences Press.

Rogers, G. (Producer, director, writer). (1978). *Soft is Heart of the Child.* [Film]. San Diego, Cal. Kroc Foundation.

Sandor, R. (1987). A physician's journey. *Parabola: the magazine of myth and tradition:* vol. 12 no. 2: 16-23.

Schaef, A. (1986). *Co-Dependence: Misunderstood-Mistreated,* San Francisco: Harper & Row.

Seixas, J. & Youcha, G. (1985). *Children of Alcoholism: A Survivor's Manual.* New York: Crown Publishing.

Singleton, G. (1982). Bowen family systems theory. In A. Horne & M. Ohlsen (Eds). *Family Counseling and Therapy.* Itasca, Ill.: F. E. Peacock Publishers. 75-111.

Small, J. (1982). Burnout seen as problem for alcohol counselors. *National Institute on Alcohol Abuse and Alcoholism (NIAAA) Information and Feature Service IFS #96,* p. 3.

Smith, J. & Gorski, T. (1985a). *Co-dependent Progression.* Hazel Crest, Ill.: The CENAPS Corporation.

Smith, J. & Gorski, T. (1985b). *Co-dependent Recovery.* Hazel Crest, Ill.: The CENAPS Corporation.

Smith, J., Gorski, T. & Miller, M. (1983). *Relapse Warning Signs for Co-alcoholism.* Hazel Crest, Ill.: The CENAPS Corporation.

Steiner, C. (1971). *Games Alcoholics Play.* New York: Grove Press.

Steiner, C. (1979). *Healing Alcoholism.* New York: Grove Press.

Stillson, K. & Katz, C. (1986). Dealing with staff burnout and countertransference. *Digest of Addiction Theory and Application:* vol. 6 no. 1: 25-32.

Subby, R. & Friel, J. (1984). *Co-dependency and Family Rules.* (available from [Health Communications, Pompano Beach, Florida]).

Vaillant, G. (1983). *The Natural History of Alcoholism.* Cambridge, Mass.: Harvard University Press.

Valle, S. (1979). Burnout: occupational hazard for counselors. *Alcohol Health and Research World:* vol. 3 no. 3: 10-14.

Wegscheider, S. (1981). *Another Chance; Hope and Health for the Alcoholic Family.* Palo Alto, Cal.: Science and Behavior Books.

Wegscheider, S. (1982). Lecture at Family Reconstruction Workshop, San Francisco.

Wegscheider, S. (1984). The untreated co-dependent as a professional. *Focus on Family and Chemical Dependency:* vol. 7 no. 2: 27A.

Wegscheider-Cruse, S. (1985). *Choicemaking.* Pompano Beach: Health Communications, Inc.

White, W. (1983). Taking care of the treatment family. *Focus on Alcohol and Drug Issues:* vol. 6 no. 4: 4, 31.

Woititz, J. (1983). *Adult Children of Alcoholics.* Hollywood, Fl: Health Communications.

Wurmser, L. (1978). *The Hidden Dimension: Psychodynamics in Compulsive Drug Use.* New York: Jason Aronson.

Wurmser, L. (1974). Psychoanalytic considerations of the etiology of compulsive drug use. *Journal of the American Psychoanalytic Association:* vol. 22 no. 4: 820-843.

Appendix 1

Children of Alcoholics Screening Test (CAST)

Pilat & Jones (1985)

Please answer yes or no to the following questions in describing your feelings, behavior, and experiences related to a parent's alcohol use. Take your time and be as accurate as possible. A scoring key appears at the end of the test.

1. Have you ever thought that one of your parents had a drinking problem?

2. Have you ever lost sleep because of a parent's drinking?

3. Did you ever encourage one of your parents to quit drinking?

4. Did you ever feel alone, scared, nervous, angry, or frustrated because a parent was not able to stop drinking?

5. Did you ever argue or fight with a parent when he or she was drinking?

6. Did you ever threaten to run away from home because of a parent's drinking?

7. Has a parent ever yelled at or hit you or other family members when drinking?

8. Have you ever heard your parents fight when one of them was drunk?

9. Did you ever protect another family member from a parent who was drinking?

10. Did you ever feel like hiding or emptying a parent's bottle of liquor?

11. Do many of your thoughts revolve around a problem drinking parent or difficulties that arise because of his or her drinking?

12. Did you ever wish that a parent would stop drinking?

13. Did you ever feel responsible for and guilty about a parent's drinking?

14. Did you ever fear that your parents would get divorced due to alcohol misuse?

15. Have you ever withdrawn from and avoided outside activities and friends because of embarrassment and shame over a parent's drinking problem?

16. Did you ever feel caught in the middle of an argument or fight between a problem drinking parent and your other parent?

17. Did you ever feel that you made a parent drink alcohol?

18. Have you ever felt that a problem drinking parent did not really love you?

19. Did you ever resent a parent's drinking?

20. Have you ever worried about a parent's health because of his or her alcohol use?

21. Have you ever been blamed for a parent's drinking?

22. Did you ever think your father was an alcoholic?

23. Did you ever wish your home could be more like the homes of your friends who did not have a parent with a drinking problem?

24. Did a parent ever make promises to you that he or she did not keep because of drinking?

25. Did you ever think your mother was an alcoholic?

26. Did you ever wish that you could talk to someone who could understand and help the alcohol-related problems in your family?

27. Did you ever fight with your brothers and sisters about a parent's drinking?

28. Did you ever stay away from home to avoid the drinking parent or your other parent's reaction to the drinking?

29. Have you ever felt sick, cried, or had a "knot" in your stomach after worrying about a parent's drinking?

30. Did you ever take over any chores and duties at home that were usually done by a parent before he or she developed a drinking problem?

SCORING: Each question is worth 1 point for a yes answer. Total the number of yes answers.

00 - 02 = probably not from home with an alcohol problem

03 - 05 = from home where alcohol created problems, but where alcoholism could not be diagnosed

06 - 30 = Child of an Alcoholic

Appendix 2

Friel Co-Dependency Assessment Inventory

Friel (1985)

Below are a number of questions dealing with how you feel about yourself, your life, and those around you. As you answer each question, be sure to answer honestly, but do not spend too much time dwelling on any one question. There are no right or wrong answers. Take each question as it comes, and answer as you usually feel.

1. I make enough time to do things just for myself each week.

2. I spend lots of time criticizing myself after an interaction with someone.

3. I would not be embarrassed if people knew certain things about me.

4. Sometimes I feel like I just waste a lot of time and don't get anywhere.

5. I take good enough care of myself.

6. It is usually best not to tell someone they bother you; it only causes fights and gets everyone upset.

7. I am happy about the way my family communicated when I was growing up.

8. Sometimes I don't know how I really feel.

9. I am very satisfied with my intimate love life.

10. I've been feeling tired lately.

11. When I was growing up, my family liked to talk openly about problems.

12. I often look happy when I am sad or angry.

13. I am satisfied with the number and kind of relationships I have in my life.

14. Even if I had the time and money to do it, I would feel uncomfortable taking a vacation by myself.

15. I have enough help with everything I must do each day.

16. I wish that I could accomplish a lot more than I do now.

17. My family taught me to express feelings and affection openly when I was growing up.

18. It is hard for me to talk to someone in authority (boss, teachers, etc.).

19. When I am in a relationship that becomes too confusing and complicated, I have no trouble getting out of it.

20. I sometimes feel pretty confused about who I am and where I want to go with my life.

21. I am satisfied with the way that I take care of my own needs.

22. I am not satisfied with my career.

23. I usually handle my problems calmly and directly.

24. I hold back my feelings much of the time because I don't want to hurt other people or have them think less of me.

25. I don't feel like I'm "in a rut" very often.

26. I am not satisfied with my friendships.

27. When someone hurts my feelings or does something that I don't like, I have little difficulty telling them about it.

28. When a close friend or relative asks for my help more than I'd like, I usually say "yes" anyway.

29. I love to face new problems and am good at finding solutions to them.

30. I do not feel good about my childhood.

31. I am not concerned about my health a lot.

32. I often feel like no one really knows me.

33. I feel calm and peaceful most of the time.

34. I find it difficult to ask for what I want.

35. I don't let people take advantage of me more than I'd like.

36. I am dissatisfied with at least one of my close relationships.

37. I make major decisions quite easily.

38. I don't trust myself in new situations as much as I'd like.

39. I am very good at knowing when to speak up, and when to go along with other's wishes.

40. I wish I had more time away from my work.

41. I am as spontaneous as I'd like to be.

42. Being alone is a problem for me.

43. When someone I love is bothering me, I have no problem telling them so.

44. I often have so many things going on at once that I'm really not doing justice to any one of them.

45. I am very comfortable letting others into my life and revealing "the real me" to them.

46. I apologize to others too much for what I do or say.

47. I have no problem telling people when I am angry with them.

48. There's so much to do and not enough time. Sometimes I'd like to leave it all behind me.

49. I have few regrets about what I have done with my life.

50. I tend to think of others more than I do of myself.

51. More often than not, my life has gone the way that I wanted it to.

52. People admire me because I'm so understanding of others, even when they do something that annoys me.

53. I am comfortable with my own sexuality.

54. I sometimes feel embarrassed by behaviors of those close to me.

55. The important people in my life know "the real me" and I am okay with them knowing.

56. I do my share of work, and often do quite a bit more.

57. I do not feel that everything would fall apart without my efforts and attention.

58. I do too much for other people and then later wonder why I did so.

59. I am happy about the way my family coped with problems when I was growing up.

60. I wish that I had more people to do things with.

SCORING: All *odd-numbered* answers must be re-flected, i.e., reversed, before summing up for a total score. Thus if the answer is "T" to item #1, it should be reversed to "F" before adding up the total. This is be-cause half the items are worded in the co-dependent di-rection, while half are not, to control for acquiescent re-sponse sets. The total score is then the sum of all "T" answers after reflection.

    00 - 20 = few co-dependent concerns

    21 - 30 = mild/moderate concerns

    31 - 45 = moderate/severe concerns

    45 - 60 = severe concerns.

J. Friel, "Co-Dependency Assessment Inventory," *Focus On Chemically Dependent Families* 8 (Deerfield Beach, Florida: 1985): 20-21. Reprinted with permission from *Focus* magazine.

Appendix 3

Styles of Enabling Behavior Checklist

Ask your client about each of the behaviors listed under each style of behavior. The one or two styles with the most positive responses are the styles which need to be included in treatment planning and education process.

1. **Avoiding and Shielding: Have you ever...?**
   _____ Made up excuses for your partner
   _____ Threw away, hid, or destroyed drugs or par-aphenalia
   _____ Threatened physical violence
   _____ Shielded partner from crisis
   _____ Helped partner keep appearances up
   _____ Covered up for partner with family or employer

2. **Attempting to Control: Have you ever...?**
   _____ Bought things for partner to divert from drugs
   _____ Spent night at motel/hotel to get partner to quit
   _____ Spent night with friend/relative to force quitting
   _____ Stayed home from work to take care of partner's problems
   _____ Constantly reminded/preached about partner's failures
   _____ Screamed, yelled, swore, cried trying to force quitting

_____ Threatened to hurt self trying to force partner to quit
_____ Stayed away from home to get away from it all
_____ Told partner to leave then went looking for partner
_____ Used or withheld sex as way to control abuse

3. **Taking over Responsibilities: Have you ever...?**
_____ Always made sure partner was awake in time for work
_____ Began to do partner's chores
_____ Began paying all of the bills
_____ Covered partner's bad checks

4. **Rationalizing and Accepting: Have you ever...?**
_____ Believed one drug is safer than other drugs
_____ Rationalized partner's use helped keep social position
_____ Believed that drug use made partner more confident
_____ Believed drug use made partner more open
_____ Provided "first aid" for drug-related ailments/illnesses
_____ Believed drug use helped partner communicate better
_____ Believed drug use made partner happier
_____ Believed use of drugs made partner less depressed
_____ Believed drugs made partner more sexually experimental
_____ Rationalized drugs made partner more alert
_____ Thought partner was more creative when using drugs
_____ Believed partner's mental abilities improved with drugs

_____ Believed drugs helped partner's physical endurance

_____ Thought drugs aided partner's physical ability

5. **Cooperating and Collaborating: Have you ever...?**

_____ Helped partner take drugs

_____ Helped partner adulterate or counterfeit drugs

_____ Helped partner weigh and package drugs

_____ Helped partner keep accounts for sales

_____ Helped chop, crush, screen drugs

_____ Made paraphenalia available to partner

_____ Supplied other drugs to counter the effects of drugs

_____ Loaned partner money to buy drugs

6. **Rescuing and Subserving: Have you ever...?**

_____ Cleaned up partner's paraphenalia

_____ Checked/measured partner's supply to see amount used

_____ Cleaned partner's vomit after abusive episode

_____ Encouraged use at home to avoid worse trouble

_____ Began waiting hand and foot on partner